ACADEMIC ENCOUNTERS
THE NATURAL WORLD

Reading
Study Skills
Writing

Jennifer
Wharton

Low Intermediate

CAMBRIDGE
UNIVERSITY PRESS

CAMBRIDGE UNIVERSITY PRESS
Cambridge, New York, Melbourne, Madrid, Cape Town, Singapore, São Paulo, Delhi

Cambridge University Press
32 Avenue of the Americas, New York, NY 10013-2473, USA

www.cambridge.org
Information on this title: www.cambridge.org/9780521715171

First published 2009

Printed in the United States of America

A catalog record for this book is available from the British Library

ISBN 978-0-521-71516-4 Student's Book
ISBN 978-0-521-71517-1 Teacher's Manual

Cover and book design: Adventure House, NYC
Layout services: Page Designs International, Inc., Fort Lauderdale, Florida

ACADEMIC ENCOUNTERS

The *Academic Encounters* series uses a sustained content approach to teach students the skills they need to be successful in academic courses. There are two books in the series for each content focus: an *Academic Encounters* title and an *Academic Listening Encounters* title. Please consult your catalog or contact your local sales representative for a current list of available titles.

Titles in the *Academic Encounters* series at publication:

Content Focus and Level	Components	Academic Encounters	Academic Listening Encounters
HUMAN BEHAVIOR High Intermediate to Low Advanced	Student's Book Teacher's Manual Class Audio Cassettes Class Audio CDs	ISBN 978-0-521-47658-4 ISBN 978-0-521-47660-7	ISBN 978-0-521-60620-2 ISBN 978-0-521-57820-2 ISBN 978-0-521-57819-6 ISBN 978-0-521-78357-6
LIFE IN SOCIETY Intermediate to High Intermediate	Student's Book Teacher's Manual Class Audio Cassettes Class Audio CDs	ISBN 978-0-521-66616-9 ISBN 978-0-521-66613-8	ISBN 978-0-521-75483-5 ISBN 978-0-521-75484-2 ISBN 978-0-521-75485-9 ISBN 978-0-521-75486-6
AMERICAN STUDIES Intermediate	Student's Book Teacher's Manual Class Audio CDs	ISBN 978-0-521-67369-3 ISBN 978-0-521-67370-9	ISBN 978-0-521-68432-3 ISBN 978-0-521-68434-7 ISBN 978-0-521-68433-0
THE NATURAL WORLD Low Intermediate	Student's Book Teacher's Manual Class Audio CDs	ISBN 978-0-521-71516-4 ISBN 978-0-521-71517-1	ISBN 978-0-521-71639-0 ISBN 978-0-521-71641-3 ISBN 978-0-521-71640-6

2-Book Sets are available at a discounted price. Each set includes one copy of the Student's Reading Book and one copy of the Student's Listening Book.

Academic Encounters:
Human Behavior 2-Book Set
ISBN 978-0-521-89165-3

Academic Encounters:
Life in Society 2-Book Set
ISBN 978-0-521-54670-6

Academic Encounters:
American Studies 2-Book Set
ISBN 978-0-521-71013-8

Academic Encounters:
The Natural World 2-Book Set
ISBN 978-0-521-72709-9

Contents

Introduction

This Teacher's Manual provides:

- information about *Academic Encounters: The Natural World* (page vi)
- a brief description of the *Academic Encounters* series (page vii)
- an overview of *Academic Encounters* Reading, Study Skills, and Writing books (page vii)
- general teaching guidelines for *Academic Encounters: The Natural World* (page x)
- answers for the tasks in *Academic Encounters: The Natural World* and additional teaching ideas for each unit (page 1)
- photocopiable unit quizzes and quiz answers for *Academic Encounters: The Natural World* (page 89)

ABOUT *ACADEMIC ENCOUNTERS: THE NATURAL WORLD*

Academic Encounters: The Natural World is a reading, study skills, and writing text based on content taught in Earth science and biology courses in high schools, colleges, and universities in the United States. In this book, authentic materials have been used as the basis for texts that use academic content and style in such a way as to be accessible to low-intermediate students.

New Features in *Academic Encounters: The Natural World*

If you are already familiar with the *Academic Encounters* series, you will discover two new features in *Academic Encounters: The Natural World*:

- **More support for low-intermediate students**
  The Student's Book has fewer readings than its predecessors and is one chapter shorter. It has nine, rather than ten, chapters and each chapter has three, rather than four, readings. This organization allows more space for tasks that support low-intermediate students in accessing the content of the readings and in practicing academic skills.

- **Guided academic writing assignments**
  In addition to tasks in which students answer test questions, complete sentences, and write original sentences, *Academic Encounters: The Natural World* provides a one-page writing section at the end of each chapter. It provides students with an opportunity to develop their academic writing skills in an assignment related to the content of the chapter or unit. Students are guided through the writing process.

Correlation with Standards

Academic Encounters: The Natural World introduces students to topics and skills recognized in the United States secondary school standards for Earth science and biology. For more information about the standards, go to www.cambridge.org/us/esl/academicencounters.

TOEFL® iBT Skills

Like the other *Academic Encounters* books, *Academic Encounters: The Natural World* provides tasks that teach academic skills tested on the TOEFL® iBT test. For a complete list of the tasks taught, see the Task Index on page 216 of the Student's Book.

ABOUT THE *ACADEMIC ENCOUNTERS* SERIES

This content-based series is for students who need to improve their academic skills for further study. The series consists of *Academic Encounters* books that help students improve their reading, study skills, and writing, and *Academic Listening Encounters* books that help students improve their listening, note-taking, and discussion skills. The Reading books and Listening books are published as pairs, and each pair focuses on a subject commonly taught in academic courses:

- Topics in Earth science and biology
   Academic Encounters: The Natural World
   Academic Listening Encounters: The Natural World

- Topics in American history and culture
   Academic Encounters: American Studies
   Academic Listening Encounters: American Studies

- Topics in sociology
   Academic Encounters: Life in Society
   Academic Listening Encounters: Life in Society

- Topics in psychology and human communications
   Academic Encounters: Human Behavior
   Academic Listening Encounters: Human Behavior

A Reading book and a Listening book with the same content focus may be used independently, or they may be used together to teach a complete four-skills course in English for Academic Purposes.

OVERVIEW OF *ACADEMIC ENCOUNTERS* READING, STUDY SKILLS, AND WRITING BOOKS

The approach

Academic Encounters adopts a content-based approach to the study of academic English. Students read through the texts, seemingly with the prime purpose of understanding the content. In fact, as students work with the text by doing the accompanying tasks, they are also learning reading skills, study skills, and test-preparation strategies. Additionally, the texts are used for language study, so students become familiar with the vocabulary and sentence structures used in academic discourse.

Each unit of an *Academic Encounters* book focuses on some aspect of the book's content focus. The fact that the book is focused on a content theme has several advantages. First, it gives students a realistic experience of studying in an academic course, in which each week's assignments are related to and build on each other. Second, as language and concepts recur, students begin to feel that the texts are getting easier, building their confidence as readers of academic text. Finally, after studying with an *Academic Encounters* book, students may feel that they have enough background in the content area (for example, Earth science or biology) to take an academic course in that subject as part of their general education requirements.

In the high-intermediate to advanced Reading books, students are presented with authentic samples of academic text. The material has been abridged and occasionally reorganized, but on the sentence level, little of the language has been changed. In *Academic Encounters: The Natural World* and *Academic Encounters: American Studies*, authentic materials have been used as the basis for texts that use academic content and style in ways that are accessible to low-intermediate and intermediate students, respectively. In all the Reading, Study Skills, and Writing books, students use the texts to develop their reading and study skills, and the high-interest content of the texts provides stimulus for writing assignments.

The content

The topics and texts in each chapter were chosen both for their importance to the theme of the book and for their appeal to students. It is important for students to be interested in what they are reading about and studying and for them to be able to make personal connections to it. According to language acquisition theory, language development occurs more readily under such conditions. Similarly, it can be argued that the writing process is facilitated when students are well informed on a topic, have developed personal connections to it, and are engaged by it.

The skills

The main goal of the *Academic Encounters* Reading, Study Skills, and Writing books is to give students the skills and the confidence to approach an academic text, read it efficiently and critically, and take notes that extract the main ideas and key details. But the goal of academic reading is not just to retrieve information. It is also important for a student to be able to display that knowledge in a writing assignment or a test-taking situation. For this reason, tasks that develop test-preparation and writing skills appear throughout the books. A longer writing assignment is at the end of each chapter.

Student interaction

To make the *Academic Encounters* Reading, Study Skills, and Writing books as lively as possible, student interaction has been built into most activities. Thus, although the books focus on reading, study skills, and writing, speaking activities abound. Students discuss the content of the texts; they work collaboratively to solve task problems; they compare answers in pairs or small groups; and sometimes they perform role plays.

Order of units

In terms of reading topics and vocabulary, the order of units is regarded as optimal. In addition, tasks build upon each other so that, for example, a note-taking task may draw on information that was offered in an earlier unit. However, teachers who want to present the units out of order may do so. The Task Index at the back of the Student's Book shows the types of tasks that have been presented in earlier units, so teachers can build appropriate background information from those tasks into their lessons.

Course length

Each unit of a Reading, Study Skills, and Writing book contains a unit preview section and six to eight readings and represents approximately 16–24 hours of classroom material, depending on the level of the students. The course can be made shorter or longer – teachers may choose not to do every task in the book and to assign some tasks and texts as homework, rather than do them in class. To lengthen the course, teachers may choose to supplement the book with content-related material from their own files and to spend more time developing students' writing skills.

Task pages and text pages

Task pages are clearly differentiated from text pages by a colored vertical bar that runs along the outside edge of the page. The text pages have been designed to look like standard textbook pages. The text is in a column that takes up only two-thirds of the page, thus allowing space in the margins for glossed terms and illustrations. Figures, tables, and boxed inserts with additional information are included on the text pages, just as they are in standard textbooks. This authentic look helps to create a sense for students that they are actually reading from an academic textbook.

Task commentary boxes and task index

When a task type occurs for the first time in the book, it is usually headed by a colored commentary box that points out which skill is being practiced and why it is important. When the task occurs again later in the book, it may be accompanied by another commentary box as a reminder, or to present new information about the skill. At the back of the book, there is an alphabetized index of all the tasks. Page references in boldface indicate tasks that are headed by commentary boxes.

GENERAL TEACHING GUIDELINES FOR *ACADEMIC ENCOUNTERS: THE NATURAL WORLD*

Each of the four units is organized as follows:

• a unit title page

• a Previewing the unit page

• a Unit contents page

• two chapters (Units 1–3) or three chapters (Unit 4), each of which contains three readings with accompanying tasks

• a unit content quiz (photocopiable pages in this Teacher's Manual)

Each of the nine chapters is divided into the following sections:

• Preparing to read

• Now read

• After you read

• Writing assignment

The remainder of this section contains general teaching guidelines for each element. See pages 1–88 of this Teacher's Manual for answers to the tasks and additional teaching ideas for each unit.

Unit title page

Each unit title page contains the title of the unit, a large illustration or photograph that is suggestive of the content of the unit, and a brief paragraph that summarizes the unit. This page is intended to look like a typical unit opening page in an academic course book.

Look at the title of the unit with students and make sure they understand what it means. Then look at the picture and have students describe it and attempt to relate it to the title. Help them with vocabulary as necessary.

Finally, look at the summary paragraph at the bottom of the page. Read it with your students and check to be sure that they understand the vocabulary and key concepts. At this point, it is not necessary to introduce the unit topics in any depth, since the unit preview activities that follow will achieve this goal.

Previewing the unit

Following the unit title page is a two-page spread. On the right-hand side is a contents page listing the titles of the chapters in the unit and the titles of the three texts in each chapter. This page resembles the typical chapter or unit contents page of an academic textbook. On the left-hand page of the spread are tasks that relate to the titles on the facing contents page. These tasks preview the unit either by having students predict what information might be found in each section or by giving them some information from the unit and having them respond to it. In this way, students are given an overview of the unit before they start reading it in order to generate interest in its content. Furthermore, students are taught the important reading strategy of previewing the titles and headings of long readings.

Preparing to read

In this book, prereading is regarded as a crucial step in the reading process. Prereading activities serve three main functions:

1 They familiarize students with the content of the reading, arouse their interest, and activate any prior knowledge of the topic.

2 They introduce students to reading attack strategies, giving them tools to be used when they undertake future reading assignments.

3 They expose students to some of the language in the text – both the structures and the vocabulary – making the text easier to process when they actually read it.

Although one or two prereading tasks are always included for each text, you should look for ways to supplement these tasks with additional prereading activities. As you and your students work through the book, students become exposed to more and more prereading strategies. Having been introduced to these, students should be adding them to their repertoire, and you should encourage their regular use. For example, after having practiced the prereading strategies of examining graphic material, previewing headings, and skimming, students should ideally carry out these operations before each and every text.

In general, the lower the level of students' reading and overall language proficiency, the more important extensive prereading becomes. The more prereading tasks they undertake, the easier it is for students to access the text when it comes time for them to do a closer reading.

Now read

At the bottom of each "Preparing to read" page is an instruction that tells students to read the text. This is a deceptively simple instruction that raises an important question: How closely should students read the text at this point? Some students, after doing prereading tasks, believe that now they should read slowly and carefully. But students should be discouraged from doing this. For one thing, it is a poor use of class time to have students poring silently over a text for 20 minutes or more, and more importantly, it is vital that students begin to train themselves to read quickly, tolerating some ambiguity and going for understanding main ideas and overall text structure rather than every word and detail.

To promote faster reading, this text includes several speed-reading tasks (in Chapters 3, 6, and 9), in which students try to put into operation techniques for faster reading. If students consistently apply these techniques, most texts will take between 3 and 7 minutes to read. Before students start reading any text, therefore, it is a good idea to give them a challenging time limit, which they should aim toward to complete their reading of the text.

An alternative to reading every text in class is to assign some of the longer texts as homework. When you do this, you should do the prereading tasks in class at the end of the lesson and then start the next class by having students quickly skim the text before moving on to the "After you read" tasks.

After you read

These tasks are of many different types and serve several different functions. You should not expect to find many conventional reading comprehension tasks. Instead, students are often asked to demonstrate their understanding of a text in less direct ways, such as vocabulary comprehension, language focus, study skills, and test-preparation tasks. Each task is intended as an opportunity to develop a skill, not simply to test comprehension.

Postreading tasks serve the following main functions:

1 They have students read for meaning, look for main ideas, think critically about the text, or look for inferences.

2 They ask students to think about the content, find a personal connection to it, or apply new information in some way.

3 They highlight some of the most salient language in the text, either vocabulary or grammatical structures, and have students use that language in some way.

4 They develop students' study skills repertoire by teaching them, for example, how to highlight a text, take notes, and summarize.

5 They develop students' test-preparation skills by asking them to assess what they would need to do if they were going to be tested on the text.

The end-of-chapter writing assignments

At the end of each chapter, students do an academic writing assignment based on the content of the chapter or unit. The difficulty of the assignments progresses from writing a list of sentences on a topic to writing one or two paragraphs on the topic. In each assignment, students are guided through the writing process.

The content quizzes

At the back of this Teacher's Manual are four content quizzes, one for each unit. Each quiz contains a mixture of true/false, multiple choice, and short-answer questions.

Planet Earth

Unit title page (Student's Book pg. 1)

Ask students to look at the photograph and think about how they would describe our planet. Give them time to read the unit summary paragraph, and check to make sure they understand the areas the unit will cover. Discuss the meanings of the words *physical*, *universe*, and *unique*.

Previewing the unit (Student's Book pg. 2)

Chapter 1: The Physical Earth

1 | Sample answers
  1 Earth is the only planet that has life, water, and air. Earth is our home.
  2 Earth provides us with food, water, air, light, building materials, and comfortable weather.

Chapter 2: The Dynamic Earth

1 | Sample answers
  • Earth moves as it travels around the sun.
  • Earth turns on its axis (it makes one turn every 24 hours).
  • Earthquakes can make the ground shake.
  • The movement of tectonic plates causes parts of Earth to move.

2 | Sample answers
  • Some landforms are hills, valleys, plains, cliffs, islands, canyons, rivers, and plateaus.
  • These features of Earth's surface were formed by the movements of wind, water, ice, glaciers, volcanoes, earthquakes, and tectonic plates.

The Physical Earth

1 | OUR SOLAR SYSTEM

Preparing to read (Student's Book pg. 4)

THINKING ABOUT THE TOPIC BEFORE YOU READ

Students are not expected to know the answers to these items. It is simply a way to get them to start thinking about the issues addressed in the text.

Sample answers

1 During the day, we see the sun, airplanes, clouds, birds, rain, and snow.

2 At night, we see the moon, stars, planets, airplane lights, and meteors (shooting stars).

3 Answers will vary.

PREVIEWING ART IN THE TEXT

1 | **Answers**

1 There are eight planets: Mercury, Venus, Earth, Mars, Jupiter, Saturn, Uranus, and Neptune.

2 Earth is the third planet from the sun.

2 | **Answers**

1 The planets are sitting and eating at two tables.

2 Pluto is talking.

3 Pluto is too small to be a planet, so it is in a different group. The cartoonist shows this by putting Pluto at the "children's table."

Now read

Refer to pages xi–xii of this Teacher's Manual for suggestions about ways in which students can read the text.

After you read (Student's Book pg. 7)

Task 1 ASKING AND ANSWERING QUESTIONS ABOUT A TEXT

1 | Answers

   1 There are eight planets in our solar system.

   2 *Orbit* means "circle."

   3 The sun is a star.

   4 Sample questions
   - What is the center of our solar system? (the sun)
   - In addition to planets and the sun, what other objects are in our solar system? (moons)

2,3 | Answers will vary.

Task 2 BUILDING VOCABULARY: WORDS FROM LATIN AND GREEK

1 | Answers

terr-: terrestrial

sol-: solar

astro-: astronomers, astronomy, astronomical

2 | Answers

Word part from Latin or Greek	Meaning	English example	Meaning
terr-	earth, land	terrestrial	relating to Earth
sol-	sun	solar	relating to the sun
astro-	star	astronomer	a scientist who studies stars and planets

Task 3 BUILDING VOCABULARY: CLUES THAT SIGNAL DEFINITIONS

1 | Answers

   1 orbit, or circle

   2 star, that is, a giant ball of hot gases

   3 terrestrial, or Earth-like

   4 astronomers (scientists who study the stars and planets)

2 | Answers

   1 star

   2 Astronomers

   3 terrestrial

   4 orbit

3 | Sample sentences

    1 A telescope (an instrument that makes faraway objects look larger) is an important tool for an astronomer.

    2 Earth is part of a solar system, that is, a star and the planets that move around it.

    3 Mercury (the planet closest to the sun) is a terrestrial planet.
       Pluto, or the plutoid discovered in 1930, is much smaller than Jupiter.

    4 Jupiter is a gas giant planet, that is, a planet made of gases, not solid rock.

Task 4 LANGUAGE FOCUS: PARTS OF SPEECH

1 | Answers

Our home in the universe is planet Earth. It is one of (eight) planets that orbit, or circle, the sun. The sun is a star, that is, a (giant) ball of (hot) gases. It is the center of our (solar) system. There are billions of (other) stars in the sky, but the sun is the star (closest) to Earth. Our (solar) system also includes moons, which orbit planets. The moon we see in the (night) sky orbits Earth.

2 | Answers

>   n.   v.   adj.   n.   n.   v. adj.   n.   v.
>   Mars is an interesting planet. In some ways, it is similar to Earth. It has
>   n.   n.   v.   n.   n.   n. v.
> weather and seasons. It also has canyons and mountains. However, Mars is a
>   adj.   n.   n.   v.   adj.   n.   v.
> very different planet from Earth. It is much smaller than Earth, and it is much
>   adj.   n.   v.   n.   n.
> colder. In addition, scientists have (not) found any life on Mars.

3 | Answers

verb	**1**		_noun_	**4**
adjective	**2**		_verb_	**5**
noun	**3**			

4 | Sample answers

    1 has   **4** moon
    2 terrestrial   **5** believe / think
    3 rings

Task 5 LANGUAGE FOCUS: COMPARATIVE ADJECTIVES

1 | Answers

seven: larger, bigger, smaller, farther, colder, darker, more irregular

2 | Answers

    1 darker   **5** smaller
    2 hotter   **6** bigger
    3 more solid   **7** stronger
    4 icier   **8** rockier

3 | Answers

1 farther . . . than
2 colder than
3 hotter than
4 closer . . . than
5 rockier than
6 larger than

4 | Sample sentences

1 Jupiter is bigger than Pluto.
2 Pluto is colder than Jupiter.
3 Jupiter has a more regular orbit than Pluto.
4 Jupiter is closer to Earth than Pluto.

2 EARTH'S FOUR SYSTEMS

Preparing to read (Student's Book pg. 12)

PREVIEWING KEY PARTS OF A TEXT

2 | Answers

1 Earth has four systems.
2 lithosphere, hydrosphere, atmosphere, biosphere

3 |

Name of the system	Key feature(s)
lithosphere	Earth's crust and the top layer of the mantle
hydrosphere	water
atmosphere	air
biosphere	living things

Now read

Refer to pages xi–xii of this Teacher's Manual for suggestions about ways in which students can read the text.

After you read (Student's Book pg. 15)

Task 1 HIGHLIGHTING

1 | Sample highlights

• lithosphere: Earth's crust and the top layer of the mantle

• hydrosphere: all the water on Earth

• atmosphere: the air surrounding Earth

• biosphere: all the living things on Earth

- We humans are part of the biosphere, but we live on the lithosphere.
- We depend on the atmosphere for air to breathe and the hydrosphere for water to drink.
- Driving a car contributes to air pollution in the atmosphere . . . . Air pollution causes Earth to grow warmer. Warmer temperatures cause important changes in the hydrosphere . . . . These changes affect the humans, animals, and plants of the biosphere.

Task 2 BUILDING VOCABULARY: WORDS FROM LATIN AND GREEK

1 | **Answers**

<u>c</u> **1**   <u>d</u> **3**

<u>a</u> **2**   <u>b</u> **4**

2 | **Answers**

1 circle   **4** gases

2 rocks   **5** living things

3 water

3 | **Answers**

- lith o(logy), atmospher o(logy)
- -*logy* means "the study of something"

Task 3 BUILDING VOCABULARY: LEARNING VERBS WITH THEIR PREPOSITIONS

1 | **Answers**

1 from   **4** on

2 from   **5** to

3 with

2 | **Answers**

1 Scientists use the Internet to connect <u>with</u> <u>other scientists all over the world</u>.

2 Sunscreen and sunglasses protect people <u>from</u> <u>the sun's dangerous rays</u>.

3 The temperature on Pluto ranges <u>from</u> <u>–238°C to –228°C</u>.

4 Polar bears depend <u>on</u> <u>a cold environment</u>.

5 Drinking clean water and breathing clean air contribute <u>to</u> <u>good health</u>.

3 | **Sample answers**

1 I depend <u>on my family</u>.

2 The summer temperature where I live ranges <u>from 27°C to 35°C</u>.

3 I want to contribute <u>to peace in the world</u>.

Task 4 USING A PIE CHART TO ORGANIZE STATISTICS

2 | **Sample answers**

Water on Earth

97% salt water

3% freshwater

- Approximately 3 percent of water on Earth is freshwater.
- Approximately 97 percent of water on Earth is salt water.

3, 4 | Answers will vary.

③ ROCKS ON OUR PLANET

Preparing to read (Student's Book pg. 18)

THINKING ABOUT THE TOPIC BEFORE YOU READ

Students are not expected to know the answers to these items. It is simply a way to get them to start thinking about the issues addressed in the text.

1 | **Answers**

   1 Photos: **a** Stonehenge in England   **b** the Great Pyramids in Egypt
      c Machu Picchu in Peru

   2 They are all made of rock.

  Sample answers

   3 the Taj Mahal in India, the Parthenon in Greece, the Great Wall in China, El Tajín in Mexico

   4 People use rocks for building, tools, sculpture, and landscaping in gardens.

  5, 6 Answers will vary.

Now read

Refer to pages xi–xii of this Teacher's Manual for suggestions about ways in which students can read the text.

After you read (Student's Book pg. 21)

Task 1 TEST TAKING: ANSWERING MULTIPLE CHOICE QUESTIONS

  Answers

1 d	**4** c
2 a	**5** b
3 d	**6** b

Task 2 LABELING DIAGRAMS

1 | Answers

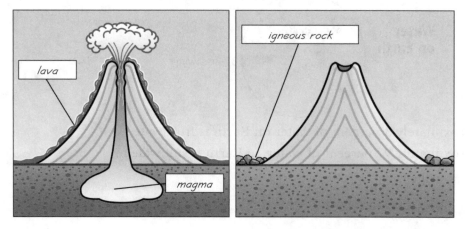

2 | Answers

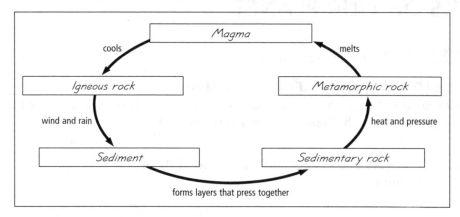

Task 3 LANGUAGE FOCUS: SUBJECTS

2 | Answers

> The atmosphere is the air surrounding Earth. It is made up of gases.
> The primary gas is nitrogen. The gases in the atmosphere create air for us to
> breathe. They also protect Earth from the sun's ultraviolet radiation.

3 | Answers

> Narenda Luther has something very unusual in his house. ^It^ Is a giant, two-
>
> billion-year-old stone. This rock is just one of many in the city of Hyderabad,
>
> India. The people ~~they~~ in the city have given names to some of the rocks. ^Some rocks^ Have
>
> become temples or billboards, but other rocks have been destroyed to make
>
> room for new development.

Corrected paragraph

Narenda Luther has something very unusual in his house. It is a giant, two-billion-year-old stone. This rock is just one of many in the city of Hyderabad, India. The people in the city have given names to some of the rocks. Some rocks have become temples or billboards, but other rocks have been destroyed to make room for new development.

Task 4 LANGUAGE FOCUS: VERBS

1 | Answers

Earth is a terrestrial planet, that is, a planet with a rocky surface. It is covered with rocks of all ages. The oldest rocks in Earth's crust are more than three billion years old. The youngest ones are just a few minutes old. All rocks are made of minerals, or inorganic (nonliving) matter.

2 | Sample sentences

1 Rocks on Earth are made of minerals.
2 Rocks are all over our planet.
3 Rocks can change form over time.
4 Rocks form in three main ways.

Chapter 1 WRITING ASSIGNMENT (Student's Book pg. 25)

Sample sentences
- Earth is one of eight planets in our solar system.
- It orbits the sun, and it has one moon.
- It is larger than Pluto and smaller than Jupiter.
- Earth is a special place.
- It is the only planet in our solar system with life.
- Earth has four interconnected systems: the lithosphere, the hydrosphere, the atmosphere, and the biosphere.
- Earth has more water than land.
- There are many different types of living things on Earth.
- Earth is a rocky planet.
- The three types of rocks on Earth are igneous, sedimentary, and metamorphic.
- The rocks on Earth change form over time.

The Dynamic Earth

1 PLATE TECTONICS

Preparing to read (Student's Book pg. 26)

BUILDING VOCABULARY: PREVIEWING KEY WORDS

2 | **Answers**

_e_	**1**	_c_	**4**
_d_	**2**	_f_	**5**
_a_	**3**	_b_	**6**

Now read

Refer to pages xi–xii of this Teacher's Manual for suggestions about ways in which students can read the text.

After you read (Student's Book pg. 29)

Task 1 USING HEADINGS TO REMEMBER MAIN IDEAS

2 | **Answers**

_b_	**1**	_a_	**3**
_c_	**2**	_d_	**4**

Task 2 BUILDING VOCABULARY: PREFIXES

1 | **Sample answers**

   1 centimeter: a unit of length equal to one-hundredth of a meter

   2 millimeter: a unit of length equal to one-thousandth of a meter

   3 converge: to come together

   4 interact: to do an action that involves something or somebody else

2 | **Answers**

   1 interplanetary   **3** convention

   2 century   **4** millennium

3 | **Sample answers**

   1 *cent-*: cents, Centigrade, centimeter, centipede

   2 *con-*: conference, Congress, connect, contact, conversation

   3 *inter-*: intercultural, interfere, intermission, international, interview

   4 *mil-*: milligram, milliliter, millimeter, millipede

Task 3 LANGUAGE FOCUS: PREPOSITIONAL PHRASES

1 | **Answers**

   Where? **1**   Where? **4**

   Where? **2**   How? **5**

   When? **3**   How? **6**

2 | **Sample answers**

   • under the oceans (Where?)

   • in different directions (How? / Where?)

   • in Asia (Where?)

   • between the Pacific Plate and the North American Plate (Where?)

   • over a long period of time (When?)

   • in dramatic ways (How?)

Task 4 READING MAPS

2 | **Answers**

   T **1**

   F **2**

   F **3**

   T **4**

   T **5**

3 | Answers will vary.

Task 5 WRITING SIMPLE AND COMPOUND SENTENCES

1 | Sample answers

Simple sentences:

- Earth is always moving.
- A good example is the Atlantic Ocean.
- This process created the Himalayas, the great mountain range in Asia.

Compound sentences:

- You may not feel it, (but) our whole planet is turning as it orbits the sun.
- He called his idea continental drift theory, (but) this idea did not explain how the continents moved.
- Today the Atlantic is a huge ocean, (and) the Mid-Atlantic Ridge is the longest mountain range on Earth.

2 | Sample sentences

- In continental drift theory, Pangaea was the name of Earth's one huge continent.
- Earth's crust is broken into many pieces, and these pieces are called tectonic plates.
- Tectonic plates are under the continents and under the oceans.
- At divergent boundaries, plates move away from each other.
- At convergent boundaries, plates move toward each other, and sometimes this movement forms mountains.

2 VOLCANOES

Preparing to read (Student's Book pg. 32)

BUILDING BACKGROUND KNOWLEDGE ABOUT THE TOPIC

2 | Answers

1 Answers will vary.

2 Sample answers: Mt. Vesuvius (Italy), Mt. Fuji (Japan), Mt. Tambora (Indonesia), Mt. Krakatoa (Indonesia), Mt. Pelée (Martinique), Mt. Kilauea (Hawaii, U.S.), Mt Llullaillaco (Argentina-Chile), Mt. Etna (Italy), Mt. Pinatubo (Philippines)

3 Answers will vary.

Now read

Refer to pages xi–xii of this Teacher's Manual for suggestions about ways in which students can read the text.

Task 1 TEST TAKING: ANSWERING TRUE/FALSE QUESTIONS

1 | Answers

<u>T</u> **1**   <u>F</u> **5**

<u>F</u> **2**   <u>F</u> **6**

<u>T</u> **3**   <u>T</u> **7**

<u>T</u> **4**   <u>F</u> **8**

2 | Answers

1 par. 2   **5** par. 3

2 par. 2   **6** par. 4

3 par. 2   **7** par. 4

4 par. 3   **8** par. 6

3 | Sample answers

2 The Ring of Fire is around the Pacific Plate.

5 Many volcanic eruptions, over millions of years, formed the Hawaiian Islands.

6 Today the world has approximately 1,500 active volcanoes.

8 Volcanoes can have both positive and negative effects on Earth.

Task 2 BUILDING VOCABULARY: WRITING DEFINITIONS

1 | Sample answers

1 A hotspot is a hole in Earth's crust that magma flows through; the lava eventually forms a volcanic island.

2 An active volcano is a volcano that is erupting now or that could erupt in the future.

2 | Sample answers

1 Tectonic plates are large pieces of Earth's crust under the continents and the oceans.

2 A ridge is a chain / range of mountains.

3 An earthquake is a movement of Earth's crust.

Task 3 READING BOXED TEXTS

2 | Answers

Yes. It gives an interesting example of an idea in the main text.

3 | Answers

- "The Story of Pluto" (pg. 6) discusses a topic that is closely related to the topic of the main text.

- "Save the Rocks!" (pg. 20) gives an interesting example of an idea in the main text. It also discusses a topic that is closely related to the topic of the main text.

Task 4 USING CORRECT PARAGRAPH FORMAT

1 | Answers

   1 The first sentence is indented.

   2 Each sentence starts with a capital letter and ends with a period.

   3 Each sentence in the paragraph directly follows the one before it.

2 | Corrected paragraph

> There are four basic types of volcanoes: shield volcanoes, composite volcanoes, cinder cone volcanoes, and supervolcanoes. Shield volcanoes are generally very large, and lava usually flows down their sides. Composite volcanoes are smaller than shield volcanoes. They can have both small eruptions and big eruptions. The smallest type of volcano is the cinder cone volcano. For example, the Paricutín volcano was a cinder cone volcano. The largest and most dangerous volcanoes are supervolcanoes, and they can cause a lot of destruction. Scientists continue to study the four types of volcanoes to learn more about our planet.

3 EARTHQUAKES

Preparing to read (Student's Book pg. 38)

THINKING ABOUT THE TOPIC BEFORE YOU READ

Students are not expected to know the answers to these items. It is simply a way to get them to start thinking about the issues addressed in the text.

1 | Sample answers

   1 The photograph shows a lot of damage to the houses.

   2 An earthquake caused the damage.

   3 Answers will vary.

2 | Sample answers

   1 An earthquake is something that makes the ground shake.

   2 Some places have more earthquakes because the tectonic plates under those places move around a lot and bump into each other.

   3, 4 Answers will vary.

   5 To stay safe during an earthquake, get away from things that can fall on you, get low to the ground, cover your head, and hold on to something.

Now read

Refer to pages xi–xii of this Teacher's Manual for suggestions about ways in which students can read the text.

After you read (Student's Book pg. 41)

Task 1 READING FOR MAIN IDEAS

1 | Answers

   1 par. 3   **3** par. 2

   2 par. 1   **4** par. 4

2 | Answers

Sentence 2 expresses the main idea of the whole text.

Task 2 BUILDING VOCABULARY: USING GRAMMAR AND CONTEXT TO GUESS NEW WORDS

2 | Answers

   hibernate   **a**

   sensed   **b**

   bark   **c**

   collapsed   **d**

   upset   **e**

Task 3 LANGUAGE FOCUS: UNDERSTANDING PRONOUN REFERENCE

1 | Answers

  1 When the tectonic plates that make up Earth's crust move past each other, they often bump or rub against each other.

  2 The pressure increases as the two plates try to move past each other but cannot. They finally move with a sudden and powerful jerk, which can also cause an earthquake.

  3 However, a strong movement can cause the earth to shake and roll violently. It can make building and bridges fall. It can also cause the earth to split open and form a large fault, or crack.

  4 The deadliest earthquake in modern times happened in 1976 in Tangshan, China. It lasted less than two minutes, but more than 250,000 people died, and more than 90 percent of the buildings collapsed.

  5 Scientists are not able to predict when an earthquake will happen. However, they can identify the areas where earthquakes are most likely to occur.

Task 4 LANGUAGE FOCUS: SHOWING CONTRAST WITH *BUT* AND *HOWEVER*

1 | Answers

1 However
2 but
3 However
4 but

2 | Sample sentences

1 Volcanoes are destructive, but they also create new land on Earth.
Volcanoes are destructive. However, they also create new land on Earth.

2 California has earthquakes every day, but only a few of them are strong enough for people to feel.
California has earthquakes every day. However, only a few of them are strong enough for people to feel.

3 Many people think Los Angeles could fall into the ocean, but this will never happen.
Many people think Los Angeles could fall into the ocean. However, this will never happen.

4 You may not feel Earth moving, but it moves all the time.
You may not feel Earth moving. However, it moves all the time.

Task 5 USING CORRECT PARAGRAPH STRUCTURE

1 | Answers

<u>Earthquakes can happen anywhere, but certain places have more earthquakes because they sit on tectonic plates that move frequently.</u> One example is the area around the Pacific Plate, which includes China, the Philippines, Japan, and the western coasts of Canada, the United States, and South America. Earthquakes are common in those places. The deadliest earthquake in modern times happened in 1976 in Tangshan, China. It lasted less than two minutes, but more than 250,000 people died, and over 90 percent of the buildings collapsed. <u>Earthquake scientists study places like Tangshan because of the many faults in these areas and the activity of the tectonic plates.</u>

TS

SS

CS

2,3 | Answers

1 Yes, the paragraph has a topic sentence.
2 There are six supporting sentences.
3 Yes, there is a concluding sentence.

There is no way to stop an earthquake, but there are several things you can do to prepare and protect yourself. [Before an earthquake happens, you should make an emergency plan. You should also prepare an emergency supply kit with a battery-powered radio, a flashlight, and enough food and water for three days. During an earthquake, you should stay away from windows and tall furniture, get on the floor, cover your head, and hold on to something until the shaking stops. If you are outdoors, find a place away from buildings and trees, and get on the ground. After the earthquake stops, check to see if you have been hurt, and listen to the radio for instructions. If you are in an unsafe building, go outside.] An earthquake can be a frightening experience, but knowing what to do before, during, and after it will help you stay safe.

TS

SS

CS

Chapter 2 WRITING ASSIGNMENT (Student's Book pg. 46)

Sample paragraph

The most beautiful place on Earth that I know is Denali National Park in Alaska. It is a great place to enjoy nature. There are green trees and colorful flowers everywhere, and you can hike for days. You can see bald eagles, bears, moose, and many other animals. They live happily and freely in the park. You can see all this natural beauty, but you do not see any pollution or trash. The air, water, and land are very clean. For all these reasons, Denali National Park is my favorite place.

Additional Ideas for Unit 1

Key topics in this unit include the solar system, Earth's four interconnected systems, and rocks on our planet. The unit also discusses the effects of plate tectonic movement, including the creation of volcanoes and earthquakes.

1 | Have students research a planet or another object in our solar system and write a paragraph about it and / or make a class presentation. Ask students to include at least one visual aid in each report.

2 | Have students research the history of space exploration and make a time line of important events.

3 | Have students work in groups and create an illustrated poster of one of Earth's four systems, including the following:
- a definition
- an explanation of why the system is important
- several important facts and statistics
- some information about threats that currently face the system

4 | Have students work in groups of two or three to identify the kinds of rocks found in their school and / or neighborhoods. Ask each group to take the rest of the class on a rock tour of the place they researched. Alternatively, have students take photographs or draw pictures and present them in class.

5 | Ask students to find information about the tectonic plates where they live. Have a class discussion about past or recent tectonic plate activity and the landforms that may have resulted from plate tectonic movement.

6 | Have students research a famous volcanic eruption or earthquake and write a paragraph about it and / or make a class presentation.

Water on Earth

Unit title page (Student's Book pg. 47)

Review the meaning of *hydrosphere* with the class. Ask students to think about the role of water in their lives. Give them time to read the unit summary paragraph, and check to make sure they understand the areas the unit will cover.

Previewing the unit (Student's Book pg. 48)

Chapter 3: Earth's Water Supply

Sample answers

1 Water features in photos: **a** lake **b** river **c** glacier

2 Similarities among water features:
- They all contain freshwater.
- They are all part of the hydrosphere.
- People enjoy visiting lakes, rivers, and glaciers.

Differences among water features:
- Lakes have land on all sides.
- Rivers flow quickly, but lake water is calm.
- Glaciers are frozen.

3, 4 Answers will vary.

Chapter 4: Earth's Oceans

1 | **Sample answers**

1 The ocean is bigger than other places for swimming. There were waves (the water moved up and down), and the water was salty. There were sharks, jellyfish, other ocean animals, and seaweed.

2 Answers will vary.

2 | **Answers**

<u>d</u> **1**
<u>c</u> **2**
<u>e</u> **3**
<u>b</u> **4**
<u>a</u> **5**

Chapter 3

Earth's Water Supply

1 THE WATER CYCLE

Preparing to read (Student's Book pg. 50)

THINKING ABOUT THE TOPIC BEFORE YOU READ

Students are not expected to know the answers to these items. It is simply a way to get them to start thinking about the issues addressed in the text.

1 | **Sample answers**

The word *cycle* means "a complete process" or "a complete set of steps."

2 | **Sample answers**

1 *Water* would be a good name for our planet, because there is much more water than land.

2 Some places where you can find water are lakes, rivers, ponds, streams, glaciers, oceans, seas, and under the ground.

3 The word *essential* means "very important; necessary, required."

4 I used water when I . . .
- took a shower (or bath)
- brushed my teeth
- washed my face and hands
- washed clothes / dishes / the car
- drank a glass of water
- cooked dinner
- watered plants

5 Answers will vary.

6 The word *decrease* means "to get smaller; to go down or become less in amount."

7 The total amount of water on Earth does not change, because the water is recycled. Water moves up from Earth into the atmosphere and back to Earth again.

Now read

Refer to pages xi–xii of this Teacher's Manual for suggestions about ways in which students can read the text.

After you read (Student's Book pg. 53)

Task 1 TEST TAKING: UNDERSTANDING TEST QUESTIONS

1 | Answers

1 How much of Earth is covered by water? The question is asking for an amount / number. (more than 70 percent)

2 How many steps does the water cycle have? The question is asking for an amount / number. (three steps)

3 Where does water evaporate from? The question is asking for a place. (from anywhere there is water and sun, such as oceans, lakes, rivers)

4 Why does water vapor change back to liquid water? The question is asking for an explanation / reason. (because it rises into the atmosphere and cools)

5 Where is the fastest water cycle on Earth? The question is asking for a place. (in tropical rainforests)

6 Why is the water on Earth today actually millions of years old? The question is asking for an explanation / reason. (because the water cycle keeps recycling the same water over and over again)

2 | Sample questions

• Why is the water cycle so slow in the desert? (because deserts are very dry and it doesn't rain often)

• Where does the water go when it falls back to Earth as rain? (some of the water goes into the ground, and some goes into lakes, rivers, and oceans)

Task 2 SEQUENCING

1 | Answers

 3 The water vapor moves up into the atmosphere.

 7 Some of the raindrops fall into lakes, rivers, and oceans.

 8 The sun comes out and begins to warm the water in the ocean again.

 4 The water vapor cools and changes into droplets of water.

 6 The small water droplets inside the cloud combine to form bigger drops, which fall from the cloud as rain.

 2 Some of the water in the ocean becomes water vapor.

 1 The sun heats the water in an ocean.

 5 A cloud forms.

Diagrams will vary, but they all should include the steps shown in Figure 3.1 on Student's Book page 52.

Task 3 BUILDING VOCABULARY: ANTONYMS

1 | Answers

_d_	**1**	_a_	**4**
_e_	**2**	_c_	**5**
_f_	**3**	_b_	**6**

2 | Sample sentences

- The temperature where I live heats up during the day, but it cools down at night.
  The temperature where I live heats up during the day. However, it cools down at night.

- My sister is the slowest runner in our family, but she is the fastest talker.
  My sister is the slowest runner in our family. However, she is the fastest talker.

- The pond near my house is small, but the lake in the park is large.
  The pond near my house is small. However, the lake in the park is large.

Task 4 BUILDING VOCABULARY: SUFFIXES THAT CHANGE VERBS INTO NOUNS

1 | Answers

1	movement	**3**	condensation
2	evaporation	**4**	location

2 | Answers

_v._	**1**	assign	_v._	**4**	evaporate
_n._	**2**	eruption	_n._	**5**	location
_n._	**3**	information	_v._	**6**	moves

Task 5 IDENTIFYING TOPIC SENTENCES

1 | Answers

Topic sentences:
- par. 2: Energy from the sun produces evaporation, the first step in the water cycle.

- par. 3: In the second step, water vapor rises into the atmosphere, where it cools and changes back into droplets (very small drops) of liquid water.

- par. 4: In the third step of the water cycle, the water droplets combine (join together) to form larger drops that fall to earth as precipitation (rain, snow, or hail).

2 | Answer

2 main idea: plants in tropical rain forests

3 Sentence c is the best topic sentence.

3 | Sample topic sentence

Earth has two very different types of deserts.

2 GROUNDWATER AND SURFACE WATER

Preparing to read (Student's Book pg. 58)

THINKING ABOUT THE TOPIC BEFORE YOU READ

Students are not expected to know the answers to these items. It is simply a way to get them to start thinking about the issues addressed in the text.

Sample answers

1 There is more salt water than freshwater on Earth.
2 More of our planet's freshwater is under the ground than on the surface.
3 Sources of drinking water include wells, water tanks, the public water supply, and bottled water.

EXAMINING GRAPHIC MATERIAL

Answers

1 Most of the water on our planet is salt water.
2 Ninety-seven percent of Earth's water is in the oceans.
3 Twenty percent of the freshwater is under the ground.
4 Seventy-nine percent of freshwater is in the form of ice.
5 One percent of freshwater is accessible.

Now read

Refer to pages xi–xii of this Teacher's Manual for suggestions about ways in which students can read the text.

After you read (Student's Book pg. 61)

Task 1 TEST TAKING: ANSWERING MULTIPLE CHOICE QUESTIONS

Answers

1 d
2 b
3 a

4 c
5 d
6 c

Task 2 NOTE TAKING: MAPPING

2 | Answers

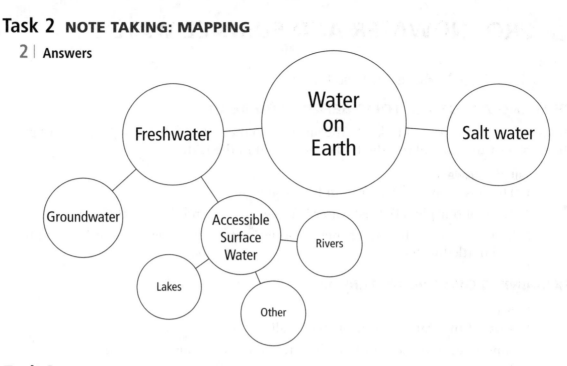

Task 3 CONDUCTING A SURVEY

Answers will vary.

Task 4 LANGUAGE FOCUS: COUNTABLE AND UNCOUNTABLE NOUNS

1 | Sample answers

The answer should include three examples of each type of noun.

- Countable nouns: liters, spaces, rocks, area(s), well, aquifer(s), cracks, lakes, rivers

- Uncountable nouns: water, rain, snow, ground, sand, saturation, groundwater, earth

2 | Answers

1 C	**4** C
2 U	**5** C
3 U	

Task 5 WORKING WITH STATISTICS

1 | Answers

1 People use more water for agriculture than for drinking.

2 Three percent of water on Earth is freshwater.

3 Most freshwater is frozen.

4 No. Not all bottled water comes from natural sources.

2 | Answers

c (80 percent = four-fifths)	**d** (20 percent = one-fifth)
f (50 percent = one-half)	**a** (25 percent = one-fourth)
e (33 percent = one-third)	**b** (10 percent = one-tenth)

1 Eighty percent of the world's freshwater supply is used for agriculture.

2 One-fifth of Earth's surface freshwater is found in Lake Baikal.

3 Almost 50 percent of the world's lakes is in Canada.

4 More than one-fourth of bottled water sold in the United States is purified water.

Task 6 IDENTIFYING SUPPORTING SENTENCES

1 | Answers
Set A

Main idea: Ways to save water

- Remember to check your home for leaky faucets.
- If any faucet is leaking, have it fixed.
- Try to take shorter showers.
- Wait until you have a full load of laundry before you run your washing machine.

Set B

Main idea: Two famous rivers

- Many people believe that the Nile River is the longest river in the world.
- It is more than 6,500 kilometers long and flows through nine countries.
- The Yangtze River is the most famous river in China.
- It is about 4,990 kilometers long and divides northern and southern China.

2 | Do not be concerned if your students' paragraphs lack smooth transitions. The point of this task is to understand the relationship between a topic sentence and supporting sentences. Future tasks will help students sharpen their writing.

Sample paragraphs

There are several ways you can save water at home. For example, try to take shorter showers. You can also wait until you have a full load of laundry before you run your washing machine. In addition, remember to check your home for leaky faucets. If any faucet is leaking, have it fixed.

Two famous rivers are the Nile River and the Yangtze River. Many people believe that the Nile River is the longest river in the world. It is more than 6,500 kilometers long and flows through nine countries. The Yangtze River is the most famous river in China. It is about 4,900 kilometers long and divides northern and southern China.

3 GLACIERS

Preparing to read (Student's Book pg. 66)

INCREASING YOUR READING SPEED

1,2 | Although much of the emphasis in this text is on reading comprehension, increasing speed is also an important goal for academic learners. Assist students by writing the start time on the board. You can ask them to write down their own finishing times, or you can write the time on the board as each minute passes. Then have students calculate their reading rates.

3 | **Answers**
1 c
2 a
3 b

Now read

Refer to pages xi–xii of this Teacher's Manual for suggestions about ways in which students can read the text.

After you read (Student's Book pg. 69)

Task 1 READING FOR MAIN IDEAS

1 | **Answers**
1 par. 4
2 par. 2
3 par. 5
4 par. 1
5 par. 3

2 | **Answer**
Sentence 3 expresses the main idea of the whole text.

Task 2 SCANNING FOR DETAILS

1 | **Answers**
1 Big Rock is located in Alberta, Canada.
2 Big Rock is 41 meters long.
3 Big Rock moved 400 kilometers.
4 A glacier creates a U-shaped valley.
5 Norway, Alaska, and Japan have fjords.
6 Glaciers cover 10 percent of Earth.
7 Lambert Glacier is the largest glacier on Earth.
8 The Kutiah Glacier is in Pakistan.

Task 3 LANGUAGE FOCUS: SUBJECT-VERB AGREEMENT

1 | **Answers**
   1 forms, turns
   2 is
   3 contain
   4 has

Task 4 EXAMINING SUPPORTING SENTENCES AND EXAMPLES

Answers

> Glaciers change the surface of our planet in different ways. One way is by shaping the land. For example, glaciers carve U-shaped valleys and form sharp mountaintops. Glaciers can also move big rocks to other locations. Another way glaciers change Earth is by creating lakes. For instance, Mirror Lake and the Great Lakes in the United States were formed by glaciers. Lake Louise in Canada is another example. Earth would look very different without the work of glaciers.

Chapter 3 WRITING ASSIGNMENT (Student's Book pg. 71)

Sample paragraph

Rivers and lakes affect our lives in many ways, both good and bad. One good way is by providing us with things we need to survive. For example, rivers and lakes give us freshwater and food. Another way rivers and lakes help us is by providing a place for outdoor sports. For instance, many people enjoy swimming, boating, and fishing. However, rivers and lakes also affect us in bad ways. For example, they often flood during heavy rains, and this can cause a lot of damage to nearby homes and businesses. In addition, sometimes the water in rivers and lakes is polluted, and we cannot use it. These are just a few of the ways that rivers and lakes influence our lives.

Chapter 4

Earth's Oceans

1 OCEANS

Preparing to read (Student's Book pg. 72)

THINKING ABOUT THE TOPIC BEFORE YOU READ

Students are not expected to know the answers to these items. It is simply a way to get them to start thinking about the issues addressed in the text.

> **Sample answers**
> 1 four (or five): Pacific Ocean, Atlantic Ocean, Indian Ocean, Arctic Ocean, (Southern or Antarctic Ocean)
> 2 Oceans are bigger than rivers and lakes; they have tides, waves, and currents.
> 3 Ocean water tastes salty.
> 4 Some living things in the ocean are fish, whales, sharks, coral, seaweed, dolphins, starfish, eels, and turtles.
> 5 Oceans are important because they are part of the water cycle; they influence climate; and they provide food, jobs, transportation routes, and recreation.

BUILDING BACKGROUND KNOWLEDGE ABOUT THE TOPIC

Sample answers
1 So many people live near an ocean because oceans are a big part of Earth (70 percent).
2 Some advantages of living near oceans are that they are beautiful and relaxing to look at; they provide recreation; and they keep the climate from being too dry.
3 When many people live near an ocean, they may pollute it.
4 If the water level of the oceans rises, it will probably cause flooding. Some people might die, and others would have to move; this would make other places more crowded.

Now read

Refer to pages xi–xii of this Teacher's Manual for suggestions about ways in which students can read the text.

After you read (Student's Book pg. 75)

Task 1 NOTE TAKING: LEARNING TO TAKE GOOD NOTES

Sample answers

Oceans

General info
    5 oceans: Pacific, <u>Atlantic</u>, <u>Indian</u>, Arctic, Southern
    Cover <u>more than 70</u>% of Earth's surface

Main oceans & features
    Pacific: largest, <u>deepest</u>, often violent
    Atlantic: 2nd <u>largest</u>, covers <u>1/5</u> of Earth's surface
    Indian: calmest, <u>smaller</u> than Atlantic

Salinity (= saltiness)
    Ocean water = 96.5% water + <u>3.5</u>% salt
    Depends on: 1) amount of <u>evaporation</u>
                    2) amount of freshwater
    Higher near the equator, lower near the <u>poles</u> & the places where <u>large rivers</u> <u>empty into oceans</u>

Importance of oceans
   Ex: 1. Role in water cycle
        2. Provide <u>food</u>
        3. Provide jobs
        4. Home for many <u>plants</u> & <u>animals</u>
        5. People like to live nearby

Task 2 USING A MAP KEY

1 | **Answers**
- Light green = less salinity
- Medium green = medium salinity
- Dark green = more salinity

2 | **Answers**
  1 L
  2 L
  3 H
  4 M

Task 3 LANGUAGE FOCUS: SUPERLATIVE ADJECTIVES

1 | Answers

six: largest, deepest, largest, calmest, smallest, lowest

2 | Answers

a largest
b coldest
c smallest

d saltiest
e most peaceful
f most important

3 | Answers

1 the deepest
2 the most violent
3 the calmest
4 the smallest
5 The most successful

Task 4 LANGUAGE FOCUS: *THEREFORE* AND *THAT'S WHY*

1 | Answers

- Together, the oceans cover more than 70 percent of Earth's surface, and they flow into each other. Therefore, from outer space it looks as if Earth has one huge blue ocean.

- When the explorer Ferdinand Magellan first sailed on this huge ocean, it was a calm day. That's why he named the ocean *Mar Pacífico*, which means "peaceful ocean" or "calm ocean" in Portuguese.

- In cold areas near the North Pole and the South Pole, there is less evaporation, and the ocean receives freshwater from melting glaciers. Therefore, salinity is lower in polar areas.

- The lowest levels of salinity occur where large rivers empty into an ocean. That's why the place where the giant Amazon River flows into the Atlantic Ocean is less salty than the rest of the ocean.

2 | Answers

_b_ 1
_a_ 2
_d_ 3
_c_ 4

Task 5 IDENTIFYING CONCLUDING SENTENCES

1 | Answer

CS: Therefore, from outer space it looks as if Earth has one huge blue ocean. (compared to TS: One nickname for Earth is the "blue planet" because from outer space, all the ocean water makes the planet look blue.)

2 | Answer

Sentence c is the best concluding sentence.

3 | Sample sentence

Clearly, Jacques-Yves Cousteau made a great contribution to the world's oceans.

2 CURRENTS

Preparing to read (Student's Book pg. 80)

THINKING ABOUT THE TOPIC BEFORE YOU READ

Students are not expected to know the answers to these items. It is simply a way to get them to start thinking about the issues addressed in the text.

2 | Sample answers

1 The wind causes ocean currents.

2 Some currents are the Gulf Stream, the Circumpolar Current, the Humboldt Current, and the California Current.

3 Currents are important because they spread the heat from the sun around Earth, they affect water temperature, and they can influence climate.

EXAMINING GRAPHIC MATERIAL

Answers

T 1

F 2

T 3

F 4

T 5

Now read

Refer to pages xi–xii of this Teacher's Manual for suggestions about ways in which students can read the text.

After you read (Student's Book pg. 83)

Task 1 HIGHLIGHTING KEY WORDS AND MAIN IDEAS

1 | Sample answers

- Currents are rivers of water that flow through the ocean.
- Trade winds are winds near the equator that blow from east to west.
- Westerlies are winds that blow from west to east between the equator and the poles.
- The Gulf Stream is a huge warm-water current that starts in the Gulf of Mexico, and then flows along the east coast of North America to northern Europe.
- Rip currents are small currents that are often dangerous because they flow quickly away from the shore and out into the ocean.

1 The main cause of surface currents is wind.

2 In general, surface currents in the ocean follow a circular path. They travel west along the equator, turn as they reach a continent, travel east until they reach another area of land, and then go west along the equator again.

3 Surface currents help spread the heat from the sun around Earth.

4 They move water in big circles, so that cold water moves to warmer places, and warm water moves to cooler places. This prevents, or stops, warm water near the equator from becoming too hot. It also prevents cold water near the North and South poles from becoming too cold.
Currents affect the temperature on land . . . . The moving water of currents heats or cools the air around them.

5 . . . the Gulf Stream . . . . begins in the Gulf of Mexico, flows past the east coast of North America, and eventually reaches northern Europe.

6 Rip currents are small currents that flow away from the shore out into the ocean . . . . dangerous because they travel very fast. . . . can carry a swimmer too far out into the ocean in less than a minute.

Task 2 LABELING A MAP

Answers

Compass labels should match those in Figure 4.1 on Student's Book page 81.

Labels on map:
1 North Pole
2 equator
3 South Pole
4 trade winds
5 the westerlies
6 Gulf Stream

Task 3 LANGUAGE FOCUS: SUBJECT-VERB AGREEMENT

Answers
1 is
2 flows
3 travel
4 blow
5 are
6 have

Task 4 LANGUAGE FOCUS: *TOO* AND *VERY*

1 | **Answers**

- Although they are small, rip currents can be extremely dangerous because they travel <u>very</u> fast.

- A powerful rip can carry a swimmer <u>too</u> far out into the ocean in less than a minute.

- The swimmer gets <u>very</u> nervous and tries to swim back to shore against the powerful current.
- The swimmer becomes <u>too</u> tired to swim anymore and then drowns.

Explanations will vary.

2 | Answers

1 too

2 too

3 very

4 very

5 too

Task 5 WRITING ON TOPIC

1 | Answers

Irrelevant sentence: ~~Ocean water is warm near the equator.~~

2 | Answers

Irrelevant sentences:
- ~~The California Current makes the climate of the Hawaiian Islands cooler than we might expect, too.~~
- ~~Peru and Ecuador are countries in South America.~~

3 | Sample paragraphs

> One of the most important currents on Earth is the Antarctic Circumpolar Current. This current flows from west to east in the Southern Ocean. Strong westerly winds blow the current around the continent of Antarctica through the waters of the Atlantic, Pacific, and Indian Oceans. The Antarctic Circumpolar Current is the largest ocean current in the world, and it moves more water around the globe than any other current. It also keeps warm ocean water away from Antarctica. That's why the ice there does not melt. These facts clearly show that the Antarctic Circumpolar Current plays an important role in the distribution of ocean water around the world.

> Like the Gulf Stream Current, the Humboldt Current has a strong effect on the climate of the land it flows past. This cold-water current travels south along the west coast of South America, from northern Peru to the southern end of Chile. Air temperatures in Chile are cooler than we would expect because of this ocean current. The Humboldt Current also affects climate in another way: It makes areas of northern Chile, southern Peru, and Ecuador extremely dry. Without the Humboldt Current, the climate in many parts of South America would be very different.

3 WAVES AND TSUNAMIS

Preparing to read (Student's Book pg. 86)

BRAINSTORMING

Sample answers

Ways oceans influence people's lives:

- Oceans provide food and jobs.
- They influence climate.
- They play an important role in the water cycle.
- They provide transportation routes.
- They provide recreation.
- They can destroy homes and kill people when there is flooding, or when storms or tsunamis happen.

BRAINSTORMING: ORGANIZING YOUR IDEAS

Answers will vary.

Now read

Refer to pages xi–xii of this Teacher's Manual for suggestions about ways in which students can read the text.

After you read (Student's Book pg. 89)

Task 1 READING FOR MAIN IDEAS AND DETAILS

Answers

M	1	D	5
D	2	D	6
D	3	M	7
M	4	D	8

Task 2 BUILDING VOCABULARY: ADJECTIVE SUFFIXES

1 | **Answers**
1 beautiful
2 enjoyable
3 predictable
4 dangerous
5 careful

2 | Answers

1 enjoyable
2 dangerous
3 careful
4 predictable
5 beautiful

3 | Sample answers

- I think hiking in the mountains is enjoyable.
- I don't like dangerous sports like skydiving.
- I am a careful driver.
- I think the ending of that movie was too predictable.

Task 3 LANGUAGE FOCUS: PARALLEL STRUCTURE

1 | Sample answers

The answer should include five examples.

> The ocean can be beautiful and enjoyable. Many people like walking on the beach and watching the water. Others enjoy swimming, surfing, and sailing. However, the ocean is not predictable, and it can be very dangerous. Wind can create big waves that knock people down, sink boats, and damage the shoreline. Giant waves, called tsunamis, can kill people and wash away entire towns. The ocean is truly a place of great beauty and great danger.

2 | Answers

1 The ocean can be beautiful and ~~enjoyment~~ enjoyable.
2 Many people like walking on the beach and ~~watch~~ watching the water.
3 The wind can create big waves that knock people down, sink boats, and ~~damaged~~ damage the shoreline.
4 The power of the ~~windy~~ wind and the waves can be deadly.
5 The tsunamis killed more than 250,000 people and ~~destroying~~ destroyed hundreds of towns.

Task 4 LANGUAGE FOCUS: *BOTH . . . AND* AND *NEITHER . . . NOR*

1 | Answers

Two sentences:

- Most waves are neither very big nor dangerous.
- The next time you go to the beach, take a few moments to appreciate both the beauty and the danger of the ocean.

2 | Answers

1 waves
2 volcanoes
3 Southern
4 preventable
5 dangerous

Task 5 WRITING THE SECOND DRAFT OF A PARAGRAPH

Completed, corrected second draft with sample topic and concluding sentences

> Duke Kahanamoku shared his love of surfing with the world, and he helped make surfing a popular sport in many countries. He was born in 1890 in Honolulu, Hawaii, and he spent his whole life near the ocean. Although Kahanamoku enjoyed swimming and canoeing, he was most famous for his skill in surfing. In fact, many people consider him the father of surfing. He traveled frequently and introduced surfing to people all over the world. When Kahanamoku was born, very few people surfed. By the time he died, surfing was a sport that millions of people enjoyed. That's why many people think Duke Kahanamoku was one of the most important surfers in history.

Irrelevant sentence: ~~He won five Olympic medals in swimming.~~

Chapter 4 WRITING ASSIGNMENT (Student's Book pg. 92)

Sample paragraph

The Indian Ocean

The Indian Ocean is one of Earth's five oceans. It is located between Africa, Asia, Australia, and Antarctica. The Indian Ocean is almost 70 million square kilometers in size. Therefore, it is smaller than the Pacific and Atlantic oceans, but it is bigger than the Southern and Arctic oceans. At the bottom of the ocean is the Java Trench, the deepest place in the Indian Ocean. The Mid-Indian Ridge is also located on the ocean floor. The Indian Ocean is usually a calm ocean, but sometimes it has storms and tsunamis. For example, in 2004 there was an earthquake in the Indian Ocean, and many deadly tsunamis formed. These facts show how the Indian Ocean is different from all the other oceans on Earth.

Additional Ideas for Unit 2

Key topics in this unit include Earth's hydrosphere, the water cycle, and sources of freshwater on our planet (groundwater, rivers, lakes, and glaciers). The unit also discusses the world's oceans, including the concept of salinity, surface currents, and waves.

1 | Have students research a particular lake, river, or other water feature somewhere in the world. Ask them to find basic facts and statistics, as well as information about the formation of the water feature and how it has changed over time. Have students write a paragraph and / or share the information in a class presentation.

2 | Have students work in small groups and collect three or four different types of bottled water. Ask them to examine the pictures on the labels and to find the words and phrases used to describe the water. Have them determine the source of the water (spring or tap). Using the labels and the information, students can make poster presentations.

3 | Have students interview people (schoolmates, teachers, neighbors) about the public water supply. Questions might include: *Do you think our town / city / country / planet might run out of water someday? Why or why not? Are you doing anything special to save water in your daily life? If yes, what are you doing?* Have students share their findings in a class discussion and / or make a class list of ways to save water.

4 | Ask students to find out if the place where they live (or have lived) was covered by glaciers in the past. If so, have them research how glaciers shaped the landscape.

5 | Divide students into small groups and have each group create a poster about one of Earth's oceans. The posters could include pictures, facts, statistics, and a few descriptive sentences. Have students share the information in a poster presentation for their classmates or for another class.

6 | Have students watch one of Jacques-Yves Cousteau's films, TV episodes, or Internet video clips. Ask them to review the show and answer questions, such as *What was the show about? What did you learn? Did you like the show? Why or why not?*

7 | Have students trace Magellan's voyage on a map. Ask them to research another famous ocean explorer, write a paragraph, and draw a map of the explorer's route.

8 | Have students determine whether tsunamis are a threat to the place where they live (or have lived in the past) and explain why or why not.

The Air Around Us

Unit title page (Student's Book pg. 93)

Review the meaning of *atmosphere* with the class. Have students brainstorm different types of climates and weather conditions. Give them time to read the unit summary paragraph and check to make sure they understand the areas the unit will cover.

Previewing the unit (Student's Book pg. 94)

Chapter 5: Earth's Atmosphere

1 | **Sample answers**
   1 Answers will vary.
   2 Some things you can see in the atmosphere are bugs, airplanes, clouds, the sun, pollution, dirt, dust, rain, and snow.
   3 Some things you cannot see in the atmosphere are space stations, satellites, and gases.
   4 Clouds can tell us if good weather or bad weather (rain, snow, storms) is coming soon.

Chapter 6: Weather and Climate

1–3 | Answers will vary.

4 | Answers will vary. (Thunderstorms are the most common type of storm. Hurricanes are the most deadly.)

Earth's Atmosphere

1 THE COMPOSITION OF THE ATMOSPHERE

Preparing to read (Student's Book pg. 96)

Students are not expected to know the answers to these items. It is simply a way to get them to start thinking about the issues addressed in the text.

BUILDING BACKGROUND KNOWLEDGE ABOUT THE TOPIC

1 | **Sample answer**
   Composition means a mixture of things that join together to form something.

2 | **Sample answers**
   1 The atmosphere is the air around our planet; the gases that make up air.
   2 The gases in the atmosphere are nitrogen, oxygen, argon, carbon dioxide, water vapor, neon, helium, methane, krypton, hydrogen, ozone, and xenon.

3 | **Answers**

   _d_ 1   _a_ 4

   _f_ 2   _c_ 5

   _e_ 3   _b_ 6

4 | **Answer**
   Nitrogen and oxygen make up most of Earth's atmosphere.

Now read

Refer to pages xi–xii of this Teacher's Manual for suggestions about ways in which students can read the text.

Task 1 TEST TAKING: EXAMINING THE LANGUAGE OF TEST QUESTIONS

1 | Answers

1 Twelve gases combine to create the atmosphere.

2 Nitrogen and oxygen are the two most common gases.

3 Nitrogen helps plants.

4 Ozone helps keep us safe from the sun.

5 Carbon dioxide prevents the air from becoming too cold.

6 The special combination of gases in the atmosphere makes life on Earth possible.

2 | Answers

1 Our air is composed of a mixture of 12 gases: nitrogen, oxygen, argon, carbon dioxide, water vapor, neon, helium, methane, krypton, hydrogen, ozone, and xenon.

2 The two main gases are nitrogen and oxygen.

3 Second, the nitrogen in the air is necessary for the plants that we grow for food.

4 The ozone in the atmosphere also provides protection by blocking harmful rays from the sun, which would burn us.

5 Carbon dioxide, for example, keeps the air from becoming too cold.

6 It is the special combination of gases in the atmosphere that allows life on Earth to exist.

Task 2 BUILDING VOCABULARY: USING CONTEXT TO GUESS NEW WORDS

Answers

_d_ 1

_c_ 2

_b_ 3

_e_ 4

_a_ 5

Task 3 LANGUAGE FOCUS: EXPRESSING PARTS

1 | Answers

• Our air is composed of a mixture of 12 gases: nitrogen, oxygen, argon, carbon dioxide, water vapor, neon, helium, methane, krypton, hydrogen, ozone, and xenon.

• The atmosphere consists of 78 percent nitrogen and 21 percent oxygen.

• Although the other gases make up only a small percentage of the atmosphere, they are very important.

2 | Answers

1 Earth's atmosphere consists of 78 percent nitrogen and 21 percent oxygen.

2 Ten gases make up less than one percent of the atmosphere.

3 The atmosphere is composed of 12 gases.

4 The atmosphere <u>consists of</u> several gases that are essential for human life.

5 Oxygen <u>makes up</u> almost <u>50</u> percent of Earth's crust.

6 The atmosphere <u>consists</u> of less than <u>one</u> <u>percent</u> carbon dioxide.

Task 4 REVIEWING PARAGRAPH STRUCTURE

Answer

Paragraph 3 has the structure of a typical academic paragraph (topic sentence, supporting sentences, and concluding sentence).

Task 5 ORGANIZING IDEAS WITH TRANSITION WORDS

1 | Answers

  _4_ **a** In addition, the atmosphere acts like a shield around Earth.

  _8_ **b** It is the special combination of gases in the atmosphere that allows life on Earth to exist.

  _3_ **c** Second, the nitrogen in the air is necessary for the plants that we grow for food.

  _1_ **d** Humans need the atmosphere for many reasons.

  _2_ **e** First, our bodies need the oxygen in the air to keep us alive.

  _7_ **f** Finally, some gases help control temperatures on Earth.

  _5_ **g** It protects us from objects that fall from space, such as meteors.

  _6_ **h** The ozone in the atmosphere also provides protection by blocking harmful rays from the sun, which would burn us.

2 | Sample paragraph

Oxygen and ozone are two gases in Earth's atmosphere that are important for humans. First, people need the oxygen in the air to survive. In fact, oxygen makes up 60 percent of our bodies. Without oxygen, we would die. In addition, people need the ozone in the atmosphere for protection from the sun. Without ozone, the sun's dangerous rays would burn us. These facts show that people could not live without the oxygen and ozone in the atmosphere.

2 THE STRUCTURE OF THE ATMOSPHERE

Preparing to read (Student's Book pg. 102)

PREVIEWING KEY PARTS OF A TEXT

Sample Answers

1 The text is about the different layers of the atmosphere / the structure of the atmosphere.

2 The atmosphere has five layers.

EXAMINING GRAPHIC MATERIAL

Answers

1 The troposphere is the bottom layer of the atmosphere.

2 The exosphere is the top layer of the atmosphere.

3 The thermosphere is the largest layer.

4 Airplanes fly in the troposphere and the stratosphere.

5 Satellites orbit Earth in the exosphere.

6 The troposphere contains living things.

Now read

Refer to pages xi–xii of this Teacher's Manual for suggestions about ways in which students can read the text.

After you read (Student's Book pg. 105)

Task 1 NOTE TAKING: USING A CHART

Sample answers

Layer	Name	Height (from ___to____)	Special features
1	troposphere	from Earth's surface to 12 km	• all living things here • where weather conditions are
2	stratosphere	from 12 km to 50 km	• no wind or weather • ozone layer here
3	mesosphere	from 50 km to 80 km	• coldest layer • meteors burn up here
4	thermosphere	from 80 km to 550 km	• hottest layer • International Space Station here
5	exosphere	from 550 km to ?	• satellites in this layer • air is very thin

Task 2 BUILDING VOCABULARY: HAVING FUN WITH WORDS

Sample answers

1 bird (other words name nonliving things)

2 tree (other words name things that can fly)

3 shuttle (other words name things found in nature)

4 pilot (other words name things that can go up into space)

5 thunder (other words name weather conditions you can see)

6 atmosphere (other words name layers of the atmosphere)

Task 3 PUNCTUATION: COLONS, *SUCH AS*, AND LISTS

1 | Answers

Lists that follow a colon:
- Scientists divide the atmosphere into five layers: the troposphere, the stratosphere, the mesosphere, the thermosphere, and the exosphere.
- It contains all the familiar parts of our world: the oceans, the mountains, the clouds, and all living things.

List that follows *such as*:
- Because most of the water in the atmosphere is located here, it is where weather conditions, such as rain, snow, and thunder, occur.

2 | Answers

Corrected sentences:
1 There are four main types of wet weather: rain, snow, hail, and sleet.
2 There are several types of wet weather, such as rain, snow, and hail.
3 There are four main types of wet weather: rain, snow, hail, and sleet.
4 There are several types of wet weather, such as rain, snow, and hail.
5 There are several types of wet weather: rain, snow, and hail.
6 There are several types of wet weather, such as rain, snow, and hail.

Task 4 LANGUAGE FOCUS: EXPRESSING HEIGHT

1 | Answers
- The atmosphere around Earth <u>extends far above</u> its surface.
- It <u>extends from</u> Earth's surface <u>to</u> an average of 12 kilometers <u>above</u> the surface.
- It <u>starts at</u> 12 kilometers and <u>ends at</u> about 50 kilometers <u>above</u> Earth.
- It <u>extends from</u> 50 kilometers <u>to</u> 80 kilometers <u>above</u> the surface.
- The fourth layer of the atmosphere is the thermosphere, which <u>is located</u> approximately 80 kilometers <u>above</u> Earth's surface.

2 | Answers
1 The <u>troposphere</u> extends <u>from</u> our planet's surface <u>to</u> an average of 12 kilometers above the surface.
2 The <u>thermosphere</u> is located 30 kilometers above the stratosphere.
3 The mesosphere <u>starts at</u> 50 kilometers and <u>ends at</u> 80 kilometers above Earth.
4 The thermosphere <u>is</u> located <u>80</u> kilometers <u>above</u> Earth.
5 Satellites <u>are located</u> hundreds of kilometers above Earth in the <u>exosphere</u>.

3 | Sample sentences
- The stratosphere starts at 12 kilometers and ends at 50 kilometers above Earth's surface.
- The mesosphere is located approximately 50 kilometers above Earth.

Task 5 USING EXPRESSIONS OF HEIGHT

Sample paragraph

    Earth's atmosphere consists of five layers. The first layer is the troposphere. It starts at Earth's surface and ends at about 12 kilometers above the planet. This layer has oceans, mountains, weather conditions, and living things. The next layer is the stratosphere. This layer begins at 12 kilometers and ends at 50 kilometers. There are just a few clouds in the stratosphere, and it is also where the ozone layer is located. The third layer is located about 50 kilometers above Earth. It is called the mesosphere. It is the coldest layer of the atmosphere, and sometimes we can see shooting stars there. The thermosphere is the fourth layer, and it is the largest layer. It extends from 80 kilometers to about 550 kilometers above our planet. The thermosphere is also the hottest layer. The final layer is the exosphere. It is located about 550 kilometers above Earth's surface. This layer has satellites. Clearly, the five layers all have special features, and each layer is an important part of Earth's atmosphere.

3 CLOUDS

Preparing to read (Student's Book pg. 108)

BUILDING BACKGROUND KNOWLEDGE ABOUT THE TOPIC

Students are not expected to know the answers to these items. It is simply a way to get them to start thinking about the issues addressed in the text.

1 | **Sample answers**
- **a** cumulus **b** cirrus **c** nimbus
- Other types of clouds include stratus, stratocumulus, cirrocumulus, cirrostratus, cumulonimbus, altostratus, and altocumulus.

2 | **Sample answers**
- When you see fluffy, white (cumulus) clouds, the weather is usually sunny and the skies are blue.
- When you see thin, wispy (cirrus) clouds, stormy weather may be coming.
- When you see dark (nimbus) clouds, it may rain or snow soon.

4 | **Answers**
1 Water in ice takes the form of a <u>solid</u>.
2 Water in rain drops takes the form of a <u>liquid</u>.
3 Water that is neither a liquid nor a solid is a <u>gas</u>.

Now read

Refer to pages xi–xii of this Teacher's Manual for suggestions about ways in which students can read the text.

Task 1 NOTE TAKING: USING A CHART

Sample answers

Cloud name	Description	Picture
Cumulus	• fluffy, white • looks like balls of cotton • found 460–915 m above ground	
Cirrus	• thin, wispy, white • looks like a thin curl of hair • found 5–15 km above ground	
Stratus	• gray, shapeless; wide, not thick • looks like a blanket • can be close to the ground (fog)	

Task 2 NOTE TAKING: USING SYMBOLS AND ABBREVIATIONS

1 | **Sample answers**

a information	**d** plus	**g** > more than
b example	**e** rise; increase	**h** ↓ decrease
c kilometer	**f** equals	**i** % percent

3 | **Sample sentences**
- Cumulus clouds are fluffy and white.
- When you see them, it is usually good weather.
- Cumulus clouds are low-level clouds.
- They are about 460–915 meters above the ground.

4 | **Sample answers**
Cirrus clouds
- thin, wispy, white
- usually = <u>stormy</u> weather soon
- high level (≈ <u>5–15 km above ground</u>)
- b/c cold @ high level, made of ice, not <u>water</u>
- cold air moves under warm air → warm air <u>rises</u> → warm air cools
  → <u>ice crystals</u> = <u>cirrus clouds</u>

5 | **Sample answers**
Stratus clouds
- gray & shapeless
- usually ≈ 0.8 km thick & almost 1,000 km wide
- usually = rain soon
- very low level (sometimes even on ground / ocean = fog)
- warm wet air moves over cooler air → warm air to rise → cools → changes into
  water droplets that join together = stratus clouds

Task 3 BUILDING VOCABULARY: WORDS FROM LATIN AND GREEK

1 | Sample answers

1 Nimbostratus clouds are layers of rain clouds.

2 Cirrostratus clouds are layers of curly clouds.

4 | Sample answers

a telescope: a type of equipment that makes faraway / distant objects look closer and bigger

b geology: the study of rocks and the earth

c astrometry: the measurement of stars

d biometrics: the measurement of biological data

e biology: the study of life and living things

f astrophotography: taking pictures of stars

g telephoto: a picture of an object that is far away

h photometer: a piece of equipment that measures light

5 | Sample answers

astrology, bioscope, biography, photograph, telegraph

Task 4 LANGUAGE FOCUS: *WHEN* CLAUSES

1 | Answers

- Clouds form when warm water vapor in the air rises in the atmosphere.
- When you see cumulus clouds, the weather is generally good, and the sky is blue.
- A cumulus cloud forms when sunshine warms water vapor in the air.
- When you see cirrus clouds in the sky, it usually means that stormy weather is on its way.
- A cirrus cloud forms when cold air moves under an area of warm air and pushes the warm air higher in the troposphere.
- When you see stratus clouds, you might soon see rain.
- A stratus cloud forms when warm, wet air moves slowly over an area of cooler air.

Three of the seven sentences have commas after the *when* clause.

2 | Sample answers

1 When water vapor rises, a cloud forms.

2 It is probably not going to rain soon when you see cumulus clouds.

3 When children draw clouds, they usually draw cumulus clouds.

4 We call it fog when stratus clouds lie on the ground or ocean.

5 When you see cumulonimbus clouds, it will probably rain soon.

Task 5 WRITING AN OBSERVATION REPORT

Sample report

Today there are a lot of clouds in the sky. I can see at least 10 of them. Most of the clouds are fluffy, white cumulus clouds. A few of the cumulus clouds are a little gray at the bottom. Those could become cumulonimbus clouds later. There are also two cirrus clouds high in the sky. According to the text "Clouds," when you see cumulus clouds, the weather is usually good. This is true about the weather today. Today's weather is, in fact, warm and sunny, and the sky is blue. However, the cumulus clouds that are a little gray and the two cirrus clouds show that it might rain in the next few days.

Chapter 5 WRITING ASSIGNMENT (Student's Book pg. 115)

Sample paragraph

Auroras

Auroras are beautiful, colorful lights high up in the atmosphere. Auroras appear in the thermosphere, from 100 to 300 kilometers or more above Earth. They usually look green-yellow, but sometimes they are red, blue, and violet. They also appear in different shapes and sizes. Auroras form when particles from the sun combine with the atmospheric gases above the North and South poles. There are two famous examples of auroras. *Aurora borealis* (Northern Lights) is best seen from Alaska, eastern Canada, and Iceland in September, October, and March. Another example is *aurora australis* (Southern Lights). This aurora is best seen from Antarctica. If you are lucky, you may see an aurora one day and be able to enjoy these beautiful lights of nature in the night sky.

Chapter 6

Weather and Climate

1 CLIMATES AROUND THE WORLD

Preparing to read (Student's Book pg. 116)

THINKING ABOUT THE TOPIC BEFORE YOU READ

Students are not expected to know the answers to these items. It is simply a way to get them to start thinking about the issues addressed in the text.

Sample answers

1 | Some words that describe weather are *rainy, snowy, humid, dry, breezy, warm, cool, wet, chilly, stormy,* and *sunny.*

2 | Today the weather is cold and rainy. It is also a little windy.

3 | The weather in the photograph is warm and sunny.

4 | The weather in the photograph looks warm and sunny, but where I live the weather is usually cold and rainy.

5 |

Group 1	Group 2	Group 3
Alaska (U.S.)	Gobi Desert, China	Hawaii (U.S.)
Nord, Greenland	Sahara Desert, Africa	Puerto Rico
Northern Canada	Rub' al-Khali, Saudi Arabia	Thailand

6 | Group 1: cold places
Group 2: hot and dry places
Group 3: hot and wet (tropical) places

Now read

Refer to pages xi–xii of this Teacher's Manual for suggestions about ways in which students can read the text.

After you read (Student's Book pg. 119)

Task 1 APPLYING WHAT YOU HAVE READ

Answers

Place	Average annual temperature	Average annual precipitation	Climate
1 Manila, Philippines	27°C / 81°F	206 cm	tropical
2 Inuvik, Canada	−9.5°C / 15°F	27 cm	polar
3 Namib Desert, Namibia, Africa	16°C / 61°F	5 cm	dry
4 Yakutsk, Russia	−10°C / 14°F	20 cm	polar
5 Monrovia, Liberia, Africa	26°C / 79°F	513 cm	tropical
6 Santiago, Chile	14°C / 57°F	38 cm	mild

Task 2 BUILDING VOCABULARY: DEFINING KEY WORDS

Answers

<u>c</u> **1**

<u>d</u> **2**

<u>e</u> **3**

<u>a</u> **4**

<u>b</u> **5**

Task 3 UNDERSTANDING AVERAGES

2 | **Answer**

The average annual temperature in Buenos Aires, Argentina is 16.3° Celsius (61.3° Fahrenheit).

3 | **Answer**

The average summer temperature in Amman, Jordan is 25° Celsius (77° Fahrenheit), and the average summer temperature in Buenos Aires, Argentina is 22.3° Celsius (72.1° Fahrenheit).

Task 4 LANGUAGE FOCUS: INTRODUCING EXAMPLES

1 | **Answers**

- For example, <u>tropical rain forests are located in hot, wet climates, and polar bears live in cold climates</u>.
- For example, <u>San Francisco and London are cities with mild climates</u>.
- For example, <u>air and ocean temperatures have been rising in recent years</u>.
- Scientists believe that global warming is causing other climate changes on our planet, such as <u>an increase in heat waves and more powerful storms all over the world</u>.

3 | **Text with examples included**

> Our planet is getting warmer, and people are concerned about it. Although some temperature change is natural, temperatures on Earth have increased much faster than expected in recent years. For example, over the 100 years of the twentieth century, temperatures increased by 0.5°C. However, before that time, it took 400 years for temperatures to increase by the same amount.
>
> Global warming is causing some troubling climate changes. For example, some areas are having more heat waves, others are getting heavier rain, and polar areas are getting warmer. Unfortunately, people around the world are adding to the problem by using more and more energy for heat, electricity, and transportation. Most of this energy is produced by burning fossil fuels, such as oil, gas, and coal. This increases global warming. To slow global warming and help prevent further damage to the planet, people need to make some changes in their daily lives. For example, they could recycle more things, walk more, and drive less.

2 STORMS

Preparing to read (Student's Book pg. 122)

PREVIEWING KEY PARTS OF A TEXT

1 | **Answers**

1 The text is about storms (thunderstorms and tornadoes).

2 **a** thunderstorms **b** tornadoes

2 | **Answers**

<u>F</u> **1**

<u>T</u> **2**

<u>T</u> **3**

<u>F</u> **4**

<u>F</u> **5**

Now read

Refer to pages xi–xii of this Teacher's Manual for suggestions about ways in which students can read the text.

After you read (Student's Book pg. 125)

Task 1 USING A VENN DIAGRAM TO ORGANIZE IDEAS FROM A TEXT

1 | Answers

<u>TO</u> are fast moving

<u>B</u> can cause a lot of damage

<u>TO</u> are tall, spinning clouds

<u>TH</u> happen more than 1,000 times a day

<u>TO</u> can lift houses into the air

<u>TH</u> can produce lightning and hail

<u>B</u> happen throughout the world

<u>TH</u> can cause dangerous flooding

2 | Answers

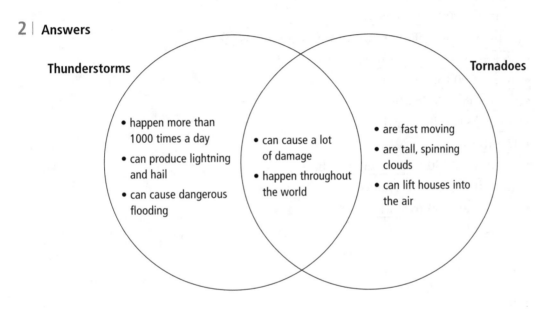

Thunderstorms
- happen more than 1000 times a day
- can produce lightning and hail
- can cause dangerous flooding

- can cause a lot of damage
- happen throughout the world

Tornadoes
- are fast moving
- are tall, spinning clouds
- can lift houses into the air

3 | Answers will vary.

Task 2 BUILDING VOCABULARY: USING A DICTIONARY

Sample answers

1 short: (adj.) happening for only a small amount of time

2 last: (v.) to continue for a period of time; to continue to exist

3 over: (prep.) more than

4 over: (adj.) finished, completed, or ended

5 strike: (v.) to happen suddenly

Task 3 LANGUAGE FOCUS: USING *THIS / THAT / THESE / THOSE* TO CONNECT IDEAS

Sample answers

1 Phrase: This movement of air
   Refers back to: The hot air expands and then quickly contracts . . .

2 Phrase: These short thunderstorms
   Refers back to: Approximately 90 percent of thunderstorms . . .

3 Phrase: Within this area
   Refers back to: "Tornado Alley," an area in the central part of the country

4 Phrase: these destructive storms
   Refers back to: severe thunderstorms and tornadoes

Task 4 EXAMINING STATISTICS

1 | Sample answers

- (almost) 2,000 thunderstorms
- (Approximately) 90 percent of thunderstorms
- (no longer than) 30 minutes
- (over) 7,000 forest fires
- (more than) 90 deaths
- (almost) $1 billion of damage
- 15 minutes (or less)
- (more than) 480 kilometers per hour
- (more than) 1,000 tornadoes
- (more than) 100 tornadoes

2 | Answers

1 b
2 a
3 c
4 b
5 a

Task 5 INCLUDING STATISTICS IN YOUR WRITING

2 | Sample paragraph

The Blizzard of 1978 was a powerful storm that struck the state of Massachusetts and caused a lot of damage and death. When the storm ended, more than 30 hours after it started, there were almost 70 centimeters of snow on the ground in the city of Boston. This destructive nor'easter destroyed more than 2,000 houses and damaged almost 10,000 more. It caused over $500 million of damage. More than 70 people died in the storm, and approximately 17,000 people had to go to emergency shelters. For all these reasons, people who experienced the terrible Blizzard of 1978 still talk about it today.

3 HURRICANES

Preparing to read (Student's Book pg. 130)

THINKING ABOUT THE TOPIC BEFORE YOU READ

Answers will vary.

INCREASING YOUR READING SPEED

1–3 | Although much of the emphasis in this text is on reading comprehension, increasing speed is also an important goal for academic learners. Assist students by writing the start time on the board. You can ask them to write down their own finishing times, or you can write the time on the board as each minute passes. Then have students calculate their reading rates.

4 | **Answers**
   1 warm waters
   2 three
   3 damage
   4 deadly and costly
   5 more

Now read

Refer to pages xi–xii of this Teacher's Manual for suggestions about ways in which students can read the text.

After you read (Student's Book pg. 133)

Task 1 READING FOR MAIN IDEAS

1 | **Answers**
   1 par. 3
   2 par. 6
   3 par. 1
   4 par. 4
   5 par. 5
   6 par. 2

2 | **Answer**
Sentence 3 expresses the main idea of the whole text.

Task 2 BUILDING VOCABULARY: SYNONYMS

2 | **Answers**
   1 refer   **4** damage
   2 start   **5** devastating
   3 powerful

- The test will begin at 9:00. It will start on time, so don't be late.
- Frogs have strong legs. They can use their powerful legs to jump very high.

Task 3 LANGUAGE FOCUS: PREPOSITIONS OF LOCATION

1 | Sample answers

1 Hurricanes form (near) the equator.
2 Some hurricanes form (over) the warm waters of the Gulf of Mexico.
3 The eye of a hurricane is (in) the middle of the spinning storm.
4 Rain bands circle (around) the eye of the hurricane.

Diagrams will vary.

2 | Answers will vary.

Task 4 THINKING CRITICALLY ABOUT THE TOPIC

Sample answers

1 Temperatures are increasing; there have been more storms lately; storms have been more severe; some places are getting too much rain, and others are not getting enough.

2 To help slow global warming, we can drive less and take public transportation more, use air-conditioning less often, and turn off lights and electric appliances when they are not in use.

3 Some reasons why people, companies, and countries have not made changes to slow global warming are people are lazy; they don't care about the problem; they don't know what to do; in some cases, it is too expensive to make changes.

Chapter 6 WRITING ASSIGNMENT (Student's Book pg. 136)

Sample paragraph

Taichung's Climate

The climate in Taichung, Taiwan is hot and humid in the summer, cooler in the winter, and sometimes rainy. During the hottest months of July, August, and September, temperatures can reach 33°C. However, in the winter months of January and February it is cooler. For example, last winter the temperature dropped as low as 22°C. The rest of the year, the temperatures are very comfortable. Another important feature of the climate in Taichung is the heavy rain that the monsoon winds bring in June, July, and August. During the rainy season, it often rains for more than a month without stopping. In an average year, about 162 centimeters of rain fall, and more than half of that rain falls during the rainy season. In Taichung, it is very hot and rainy at times, but most of the year, the weather is good.

Additional Ideas for Unit 3

Key topics in this unit include the composition and structure of the atmosphere, and the importance of the atmospheric gases. The unit also discusses some of Earth's climate zones, common weather conditions, and climate change.

1. Have students research one of the gases in the atmosphere and write a paragraph about it and / or make a class presentation. As preparation, have students review the boxed text "Oxygen" (Student's Book page 98).

2. Have students research and discuss or debate this question: *Is space travel worth the cost it requires? Why or why not?*

3. Ask students to keep a cloud log for one month in which they record the clouds and weather conditions each day. Then have them analyze their findings and write a paragraph about it.

4. Have students work in groups, and assign each group a different type of climate (hot, wet, cold, dry, and so on). Ask each group to create a travel poster for an imaginary place, including a description of the assigned climate. Instruct students to make the place and its climate sound as appealing as possible.

5. Have students create a chart of the wettest, coldest, windiest, hottest, and driest places on Earth.

6. Have students research and calculate the average temperature and rainfall for the place they live now or a place they have lived in the past.

7. Have students imagine that a powerful storm has struck the place where they live, and have them write about this "storm of the century" in newspaper-article format.

8. Have students research an alternative energy source, such as solar energy or nuclear energy, and write a paragraph about it and / or make a class presentation. As preparation, have students review the boxed text "The Benefits of Wind" (Student's Book page 132).

Life on Earth

Unit 4

Unit title page (Student's Book pg. 137)

Ask students to look at the photo collage and think about how it relates to the unit title. Give them time to read the unit summary paragraph, and check to make sure they understand the areas the unit will cover.

Previewing the unit (Student's Book pg. 138)

Chapter 7: Plants and Animals

1 | **Sample answers**
- Some living things are birds, ants, flies, flowers, trees, frogs, dogs, cats, and people.
- Some nonliving things are houses, cars, roads, trashcans, airplanes, lights, and signs.
- All living things eat, grow, and die.

2 | **Answers**

P	1		P	4
A	2		A	5
A	3		P	6

- Animals sometimes eat other animals.
- Many plants can produce flowers.

Chapter 8: The Human Body

Answers

T	1		F	4
F	2		F	5
T	3		T	6

Chapter 9: Living Longer, Living Better?

1 | **Sample answers**
- People are living longer today because of better medicine, better food, and cleaner living conditions. Human lives are better because many people are healthier, and they can stay active longer.

2 | **Sample answers**
- Bad effects of human activity include air and water pollution, which harms plants and animals; and too much development of land, which can destroy natural habitats.
- Good effects include research on renewable sources of energy and more help for endangered species.

Chapter

Plants and Animals

1 LIVING THINGS

Preparing to read (Student's Book pg. 140)

THINKING ABOUT THE TOPIC BEFORE YOU READ

Students are not expected to know the answers to these items. It is simply a way to get them to start thinking about the issues addressed in the text.

1 | Answers will vary. (All statements are true.)

3 | **Sample answers**
  • All living things are made of cells.
  • All living things reproduce (produce young).

BUILDING BACKGROUND KNOWLEDGE ABOUT THE TOPIC

Answers

Now read

Refer to pages xi–xii of this Teacher's Manual for suggestions about ways in which students can read the text.

After you read (Student's Book pg. 143)

Task 1 TEST TAKING: ANSWERING TRUE/FALSE QUESTIONS

1 | Answers

F 1 par. 2   F 5 par. 3

T 2 par. 2   F 6 par. 1

T 3 par. 5   T 7 par. 3

F 4 par. 4   T 8 par. 4

2 | Sample answers

1 All organisms need water.

4 Humans are multicellular organisms, but bacteria are single-celled organisms.

5 All cells have a cell membrane and cytoplasm, and most cells have a nucleus.

6 Fish and birds are organisms, but rocks are not.

Task 2 BUILDING VOCABULARY: WORD FAMILIES

1 | Answers

1 life (n.)   living (adj.)   4 cell (n.)   multicellular (adj.)

2 difference (n.)   different (adj.)   5 movement (n.)   move (v.)

3 similarity (n.)   similar (adj.)   6 diversity (n.)   diverse (adj.)

2 | Answers

1 different

2 cell

3 move

4 similar

5 diversity

Task 3 ASKING FOR CLARIFICATION

2 | Sample answers

1 In other words, a cell is the smallest living thing on Earth.

2 The word *circulatory* describes something that moves in a circle.

3 Some examples of organ systems are the digestive system, the respiratory system, the nervous system, the skeletal system, and the muscular system.

4 "All organisms develop" means that all organisms grow and change.

3 | Sample questions

• Could you explain what the word *nucleus* means? (A nucleus is the central part of a cell; it contains all the information a cell needs to grow and develop.)

• I don't understand what the text means in paragraph 2 where it says that life on Earth is extremely diverse. (It means that living things on Earth are not all the same. They differ in many ways, including size, shape, and habitat.)

Task 4 WRITING ABOUT SIMILARITIES

1 | Answers

par. 1: They <u>are all</u> organisms, or living things, . . .

par. 2: Although organisms are different from each other in these ways, they <u>are</u> <u>similar</u> in other ways. For example, they <u>all</u> need food for energy . . . . In addition, <u>all</u> organisms grow, develop, and eventually die.

par. 3: <u>Another important similarity is that all</u> organisms <u>are</u> composed of cells . . . . <u>All</u> cells have an outer covering, called a cell membrane.

par. 4: For example, <u>both</u> bacteria and algae <u>are</u> single-celled organisms.

2 | Answers

1 similar; similarity, all

2 both

3 Both

4 All

3 | Sample sentences

1 Both dogs and cats have tails.

2 One similarity is that whales and fish both live in water.

3 Mosquitoes and ants are both insects.

4 | Answers

1 The writer is comparing lions and tigers.

2 The three points of comparison are diet, family group, and size.

3

> Lions and tigers <u>are similar</u> in three ways. <u>One similarity</u> <u>is that</u> <u>both</u> animals have <u>similar</u> diets. Lions and tigers are <u>both</u> meat eaters who hunt large and medium-size animals. <u>Another similarity is that</u> both animals <u>are</u> part of the cat family. Lions <u>are</u> also <u>similar to</u> tigers in size. <u>Both</u> animals <u>are</u> about <u>the same</u> weight and height. As you can see, lions and tigers <u>have</u> several things <u>in common</u>.

5 | Sample paragraph

Dogs and cats are similar in several ways. First, both animals are popular house pets. They are both good companions for people. Another similarity is that dogs and cats have some physical features in common. For example, they both have hair, whiskers, four legs, and a tail. In addition, dogs and cats both eat meat. These are just a few examples of how dogs and cats are similar.

2 PLANT LIFE

Preparing to read (Student's Book pg. 146)

CONDUCTING A SURVEY

Sample answers
- Reasons that plants are important include the following: they give us oxygen; they are a source of food for people and animals; they are beautiful; and they make people happy.
- Products we get from plants include cotton clothing, pencils, paper, fruits, vegetables, herbs, rice and other grains, wooden furniture, linen tablecloths, chocolate, and coffee.

PREVIEWING KEY PARTS OF A TEXT

Answers

<u>T</u> 1   <u>F</u> 4

<u>F</u> 2   <u>F</u> 5

<u>T</u> 3   <u>T</u> 6

Now read

Refer to pages xi–xii of this Teacher's Manual for suggestions about ways in which students can read the text.

After you read (Student's Book pg. 149)

Task 1 NOTE TAKING: OUTLINING

Sample answers
I.   Diversity of plants
    A. ≈ 300,000 types of plants on Earth
    B. grow in lots of different <u>climates</u>
II. Plant size and structure
    A. different sizes
    B. plant structure: made up of <u>cells</u>, which have cell <u>membranes</u>, <u>cytoplasm</u>, a <u>nucleus</u>, and cell <u>walls</u>
III. Seedless plants
    A. grow from <u>spores</u>, not seeds
    B. do not have flowers and most grow in <u>damp</u> places
IV. <u>Seed plants</u>
    A. more common than seedless plants
    B. they have <u>roots</u>, <u>stems</u>, and <u>leaves</u>, and they can have <u>flowers</u>
V.   Products from plants
    A. provide us with food, clothing, paper, wood, and medicine
    B. most importantly, they provide <u>oxygen</u>

VI. Photosynthesis
   A. takes place in plant leaves
   B. the process: plants take in <u>sunlight</u>, <u>carbon dioxide</u>, and <u>water</u>, and they make <u>glucose (food)</u>
   C. process puts <u>oxygen</u> into the air and takes out <u>carbon dioxide</u>

VII. Plant loss
   A. causes: <u>natural disasters (fires) and human activity (cutting down trees)</u>
   B. effects: <u>loss of habitats, drought, less oxygen and more carbon dioxide in the air, so more global warming</u>

Task 2 BUILDING VOCABULARY: DEFINING KEY WORDS

1 | **Answers**

  <u>d</u> **1**   <u>e</u> **4**

  <u>c</u> **2**   <u>f</u> **5**

  <u>a</u> **3**   <u>b</u> **6**

2 | **Answers**

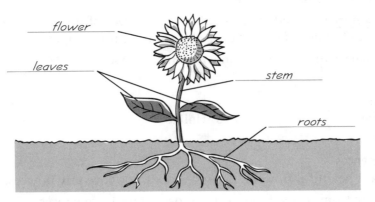

3 | **Answers**

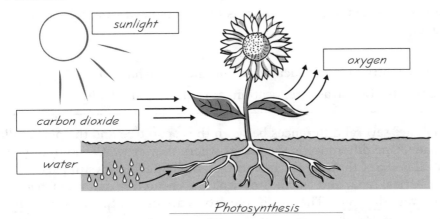

Task 3 BUILDING VOCABULARY: CLUES THAT SIGNAL DEFINITIONS

Sample answers

Word		Definition	Clue
1 spores	(par. 3)	tiny cells that grow into new plants	Spores are . . .
2 photosynthesis	(par. 6)	a plant's food-making process	. . ., called photosynthesis
3 glucose	(par. 6)	a kind of sugar	Glucose is . . .
4 deforestation	(par. 7)	destruction of trees	deforestation, or . . .
5 drought	(par. 7)	a long period of time without rain	drought ( )

Task 4 WRITING ABOUT DIFFERENCES

1 | **Answers**

par. 1: Plants are similar to other organisms in several ways, <u>but</u> they also have their own special features.

par. 2: <u>In contrast</u>, consider the giant redwood trees of northern California . . . <u>One difference</u> is that plant cells also have thick, rigid cell walls . . .

par. 4: <u>Unlike</u> seedless plants, many also have flowers . . .

2 | **Answers**

1 different
2 In contrast
3 difference
4 but
5 Unlike

3 | **Sample sentences**

• Roses have beautiful flowers, but moss does not have any flowers.

• Roses grow from seeds. In contrast, moss grows from spores.

• Unlike roses, moss often grows on rocks.

• One difference between roses and moss is that roses need sun, but moss needs shade.

4 | **Answers**

1 The writer is contrasting the cacao tree and the nightshade plant.

2 The three points of contrast are location, appearance, and fruit.

3

> <u>There are several differences between</u> the cacao tree and the plant called nightshade. <u>One difference is</u> the places where they grow. Cacao trees grow in Central and South America. <u>In contrast</u>, nightshade grows in parts of Europe, Africa, Asia, and North America. The cacao tree and nightshade also <u>look</u> very <u>different</u>. The cacao tree grows about eight meters high, <u>but</u> nightshade grows only to about one meter. <u>The most important difference between</u> the cacao tree and nightshade is the fruit they produce. Cacao trees produce huge berries called cacao pods. Inside the pods are seeds that are used to make chocolate. <u>Unlike the cacao fruit</u>, nightshade berries are poisonous. In fact, if you eat nightshade, you could die. As you can see, nightshade and the cacao tree <u>are</u> two very <u>different</u> plants.

5 | Sample paragraph

There are several differences between basil plants and pansies. One important difference is the conditions they need to grow. Pansies grow best when the weather is cool. In fact, pansies can continue to grow even when it snows lightly. In contrast, basil needs hot, dry weather, and it will die if it gets too cold. Another difference between basil and pansies is the flowers. Basil plants produce long white or purple flowers with many petals. Unlike basil, pansies come in many different colors, such as yellow, orange, purple, red, and white. Each flower has only five petals. The biggest difference between the two plants is that basil is an herb, but a pansy is not. People often use basil leaves in cooking, but they use pansies to provide color in the garden. Although basil and pansies are both popular garden plants, they look very different, and they have different needs and uses.

3 ANIMAL LIFE

Preparing to read (Student's Book pg. 154)

THINKING ABOUT THE TOPIC BEFORE YOU READ

Students are not expected to know the answers to these items. It is simply a way to get them to start thinking about the issues addressed in the text.

1 | Sample answers

1 Categorization

- animals in the air: bird, mosquito
- animals in the water: crab, fish, turtle, whale
- animals on land: cow, dog, elephant, kangaroo, ladybug, lion, monkey, mouse, spider, worm
- animals on land and in the water: crab, turtle

2 Recategorization

- big animals: cow, elephant, kangaroo, lion, monkey, whale
- medium-size animals: dog, monkey
- small animals: bird, crab, ladybug, mosquito, mouse, spider, turtle, worm

2 | Sample answers

1 In photo a, the rhinoceros and the birds are friends.
2 In photo b, the turtle and the fish like to travel together.
3 In photo c, the mosquito is biting / hurting the person.

Now read

Refer to pages xi–xii of this Teacher's Manual for suggestions about ways in which students can read the text.

After you read (Student's Book pg. 157)

Task 1 APPLYING WHAT YOU HAVE READ

1 | Answers

1 _V_ (monkey)   5 _I_ (crab)

2 _I_ (worm)   6 _I_ (snail)

3 _V_ (bird)   7 _V_ (fish)

4 _V_ (horse)   8 _I_ (shrimp)

2 | Answers

_M_ 1   _M_ 4

_C_ 2   _P_ 5

_P_ 3

3 | Answers

extinct 1

endangered 2

Task 2 LANGUAGE FOCUS: *THAT* CLAUSES

1 | Answers

- Vertebrates are animals that have a backbone.
- A backbone is a line of bones that goes down the middle of the animal's back.
- It supports the animal and protects the spinal cord, which is an important group of nerves that sends messages between the brain and the rest of the body.
- Every vertebrate also has a head with a skull that surrounds and protects the brain.
- Invertebrates are animals that do not have backbones, such as worms and spiders.
- For example, some small birds sit on water buffaloes and eat the insects that bother the animals.
- For example, sometimes a fly lands on the back of a cow that is walking across a field.

2 | Sample sentences

1 Plants are organisms that can make their own food.

2 Birds are animals that have feathers and can fly.

3 Human activities cause environmental changes that sometimes hurt other living things on our planet.

4 Some animals form relationships that they both benefit from.

5 Earth is a planet that has more salt water than freshwater.

Task 3 BUILDING VOCABULARY: COMPOUND WORDS

1 | Sample answers

1 a bone that goes down your back

2 a fish that is soft and squishy (like jelly)

3 a tree that has red wood

4 a horse that runs in races

5 a lot of ideas in a person's brain

6 the top of a mountain

2 | Sample answers

songbird, earthquake, earthworm, rainfall, rainwater, sunshine, sunflower, shellfish, thunderstorm, waterfall

3 | Sample answers

airmail, airport, armchair, backpack, ballplayer, bathroom, birthday, blackboard, classroom, cowboy, footprint, goldfish, haircut, headache, homemade, lunchroom, moonlight, tabletop, textbook, toothbrush, trashcan, snowman, sunburn, weekend

Task 4 WRITING ABOUT SIMILARITIES AND DIFFERENCES

1 | Answers

1 The writer compares and contrasts sharks and jellyfish.

2 similarities: both live in the ocean; both can hurt people and other animals
differences: sharks are vertebrates, but jellyfish are invertebrates; sharks live longer than jellyfish

3

> Sharks and jellyfish are similar to and different from each other in several ways. One similarity is that both animals live in the ocean. Another similarity is that both sharks and jellyfish can hurt people and other animals. A shark can bite with its sharp teeth, and a jellyfish can sting with its tentacles. Although there are similarities between these animals, there are also important differences. One difference is that sharks are vertebrates and jellyfish are invertebrates. This means that, unlike sharks, jellyfish do not have backbones or brains. Sharks and jellyfish also have different life spans. Most jellyfish live only a few months. In contrast, most sharks live 15–20 years. These facts show that sharks and jellyfish are similar and different at the same time.

2 | Sample paragraph

Plants and animals have similarities, but they also have differences. One similarity is that plants and animals are both made up of cells. Another similarity is that they are both organisms. That means they both need water, food, air to breathe, and a place to live. Although there are similarities between plants and animals, there are also major differences. For example, one difference is cell structure. Unlike animal cells, plant cells have cell walls. An even bigger difference is that most plants can make their own food through the process of photosynthesis. In contrast, animals have to eat plants or other animals. Clearly, plants and animals have some things in common, but they are also different from each other in important ways.

Task 5 THINKING CRITICALLY ABOUT THE TOPIC

1 | **Sample answers**

1 Some endangered animals are Asian elephants, blue whales, gorillas, giant pandas, red wolves, Siberian tigers, and California condors. Some extinct animals are dodo birds, saber-toothed tigers, wooly mammoths, giant kangaroos, giant moas, dinosaurs, Irish deer, and Caspian tigers.

2 Animals may become endangered or extinct because people kill them for food or fur, or because people think the animals are pests.

2 | **Sample answers**

1 Answers will vary.

2 Animal communication techniques include making noises (barking, meowing, growling); touching each other with their paws, noses, or faces; and bringing things to each other, such as food or toys.

3 Some ways animals communicate with people include making noise, wagging their tails, staring, and bringing people things.

3 | **Sample answer**

Dolphins communicate with each other in their own language, which people cannot understand.

Chapter 7 WRITING ASSIGNMENT (Student's Book page 161)

Sample paragraph

Cheetahs and Giraffes

Cheetahs and giraffes are two mammals that have many differences and a few similarities. The clearest difference between the cheetah and the giraffe is the size and shape of their bodies. The giraffe is the tallest animal on land. An average giraffe is about 5 meters tall. In contrast, an average cheetah is about 80 centimeters tall, but its long body and powerful legs make it the fastest animal on land. In fact, cheetahs can run as fast as 112 kilometers an hour. Another difference between the two animals is their diet. Giraffes are herbivores, which means they do not eat meat. Their favorite food is the leaves of the acacia tree. Unlike giraffes, cheetahs are meat eaters. They usually eat antelopes, birds, and rabbits. Although these two animals are very different, they do have a few things in common. One similarity is the place where they live. Both giraffes and cheetahs live in Africa. Another similarity is that both animals have short fur. In addition, they both have spots on their fur. As you can see, the giraffe and the cheetah are very different from each other, but they have a few similar features.

Chapter 8

The Human Body

1 THE BRAIN

Preparing to read (Student's Book pg. 162)

THINKING ABOUT THE TOPIC BEFORE YOU READ

Students are not expected to know the answers to these items. It is simply a way to get them to start thinking about the issues addressed in the text.

1 | **Sample answer**
Humans are unique because they are very intelligent; they have a complex language system; and they know they will die someday.

2 | **Sample answers**
The picture shows a woman's face / a man playing the saxophone.

Now read

Refer to pages xi–xii of this Teacher's Manual for suggestions about ways in which students can read the text.

After you read (Student's Book pg. 165)

Task 1 NOTE TAKING: FROM HIGHLIGHTING TO NOTES

1 | **Sample answers**
1 The main idea is highlighted in gray; details are highlighted in green.
2, 3 Answers will vary.

2 | Sample answers

Answers will vary. Check to make sure that students have limited their highlighting to important information.

Task 2 BUILDING VOCABULARY: USING ADJECTIVES

1 | Answers

Phineas Gage was a <u>railroad</u> employee. He was a <u>good</u> worker and a <u>respected</u> man. His employer thought he was <u>smart</u> and <u>responsible</u>, and the people he supervised said he was a <u>fair</u> boss. One day in 1848, there was a <u>terrible</u> accident. A <u>heavy</u> <u>iron</u> bar went right through Gage's head. He did not die, but a <u>large</u> section of the <u>front</u> part of his brain was destroyed.

When Gage went back to work the <u>next</u> year, everyone noticed <u>enormous</u> changes in his personality. Before the accident, Gage was <u>calm</u>, <u>hardworking</u>, <u>responsible</u>, and <u>friendly</u>. However, after the accident, he became <u>angry</u>, <u>childish</u>, <u>rude</u>, and <u>impatient</u>. Years later, scientists discovered that the <u>front</u> part of the brain controls personality. This explains why Gage's personality changed so much after his injury.

2 | Sample answers

1 The brain is a small organ.

2 Humans have complex brains.

3 There are different types of seedless plants on Earth.

4 Mosquitoes are annoying insects.

5 Elephants are enormous and intelligent animals.

3 | Sample sentences

It is the tallest animal on land. It has a long neck, four long legs, and a very long tongue. Its fur is yellow with brown spots. (a giraffe)

Task 3 LANGUAGE FOCUS: GERUNDS

1 | Answers

<u>G</u> 1 <u>Thinking</u> is something our brains do all day long.

___ 2 Many scientists are <u>doing</u> brain research.

<u>G</u> 3 Experts say <u>sleeping</u> is very important for healthy brain development.

<u>G</u> 4 <u>Hearing</u> and <u>seeing</u> are two senses that the brain controls.

___ 5 Scientists are <u>learning</u> more about the brain every day.

2 | Sample answers

1 The cerebrum controls most of a person's <u>thinking</u> and <u>speaking</u>.

2 The right hemisphere of the brain is important for creative abilities, such as <u>drawing</u> and <u>painting</u>.

3 The brain stem controls some of the body's basic functions, such as <u>breathing</u>.

3 | Answers will vary.

Task 4 APPLYING WHAT YOU HAVE READ

1 | Answers will vary.

Task 5 WRITING A DESCRIPTION

1 | **Answers**

1 The writer is describing the brain.

2, 3 Sample answers

> When scientists describe the brain, they note several (key) features. Surprisingly, the brain is quite (small,) even though it is (complex.) An (average) brain is about the size of two fists, and it weighs approximately 1.4 kilograms. Some people describe the brain as looking like a (soft,) (pink,) (wrinkled) rock. Others say it looks like a sponge. This (important) organ consists of three parts: the cerebrum, the cerebellum, and the brain stem.

Note that many grammarians consider amounts (*several*) and numbers (*three*) to be determiners, not adjectives.

3 | **Sample paragraph**

The human eye is round, and it is about 2.5 centimeters from side to side and top to bottom. A large part of the eye is white. In the middle of the white part is a smaller circle. This circle can be brown, green, or blue. Inside the colored circle is a smaller black circle. The eye can move up and down and side to side when it looks in different directions. Over the eye is the eyelid, which is the skin that covers the eye when it closes.

2 THE SKELETAL AND MUSCULAR SYSTEMS

Preparing to read (Student's Book pg. 170)

THINKING ABOUT THE TOPIC BEFORE YOU READ

Students are not expected to know the answers to these items. It is simply a way to get them to start thinking about the issues addressed in the text.

1 | **Answers**

a muscular system   **b** skeletal system

2 | **Answers**

B	**1**		B/M	**4**
B/M	**2**		M	**5**
M	**3**		B	**6**

1 206
2 more muscles than bones
3 thigh bone
4 cannot

Now read

Refer to pages xi–xii of this Teacher's Manual for suggestions about ways in which students can read the text.

After you read (Student's Book pg. 173)

Task 1 ASKING AND ANSWERING QUESTIONS ABOUT A TEXT

1 | **Sample answers**

1 Body movements include walking, talking, sitting, bending, blinking, and smiling.
2 Muscles and bones allow us to move.
3 A skeleton is a framework of bones inside the body. It gives the body shape and support.
4 A bone is made of living cells and tissues; it is lightweight and strong; the outside is hard, and the inside has some empty spaces.
5 Two purposes of bones are to protect internal organs and to help support the body.
6 The femur is a bone that supports the weight of the body as we walk and run.

2 | Answers will vary.

Task 2 NOTE TAKING: FROM HIGHLIGHTING TO NOTES

1 | **Sample highlighting**

Bones have two main purposes. Some bones protect the internal organs. skull For example, the skull bones protect the brain, the ribs protect the heart, ribs and the backbone protects the spinal cord. Other bones, such as the backbone femur, or thighbone, help support the body. The femur is the longest bone in the body. It is an average of 48 centimeters long, and it supports femur the weight of the body as we walk and run.

2 | **Sample notes**

Two main purposes of bones

1 To protect the body's internal organs
   • skull protects the brain
   • ribs protect the heart
   • backbone protects the spinal cord
2 To help support the body
   • femur supports body weight as we walk & run

4 | Answers will vary.

Task 3 SCANNING FOR DETAILS

Answers

1 People usually take 5,000 steps in one day.

2 My body has 206 bones.

3 An average human skeleton weighs about 10 kilograms.

4 The femur is the longest bone. It is an average of 48 centimeters long.

5 The body has more than 600 skeletal muscles.

6 It takes more muscles to frown than to smile.

7 Babies have about 300 bones. Adults have 206 bones.

8 Half of the bones in the body are in the hands and feet.

Task 4 BUILDING VOCABULARY: USING A DICTIONARY

1 | **Sample answers**

1 step: (n.) the distance covered by lifting one foot and putting it down in front of the other foot

2 tissue: (n.) a group of related cells that forms larger parts of animals and plants

3 contract: (v.) to make or become shorter or narrower, or smaller

4 relax: (v.) to become or cause a muscle or the body to become less tight

5 major: (adj.) more important, bigger, or more serious than others of the same type

6 diet: (n.) the food and drink usually taken by a person or group

Task 5 BUILDING VOCABULARY: WORDS THAT CAN BE USED AS NOUNS OR VERBS

2 | **Sample answers**

1 The femur supports the body when we run.

2 Doctors listen to a patient's heart as it beats to make sure it is healthy.

3 | **Sample sentences**

• I wish I had better control over the weeds in my garden. (noun)

• It's hard to control the weeds in my garden. (verb)

• A frown shows people that you are not happy. (noun)

• When you frown, people can see you are not happy. (verb)

• I like to take a walk with my family every night after dinner. (noun)

• I walk every night after dinner with my family. (verb)

• I enjoy my work in the chemistry lab at school. (noun)

• I work in the chemistry lab at school. (verb)

Task 6 WRITING A DESCRIPTION

1 | Sample answers

Paragraph 2 describes bones:

> Inside the body is a framework of 206 bones, called a skeleton. Bones are <u>made of living cells and tissue</u>, and they give shape and support to the body. They are both <u>lightweight</u> and <u>strong</u>. The <u>outside of a bone is hard and solid</u>, and the <u>inside has some empty spaces</u>, which makes it <u>light</u>. An average skeleton <u>weighs only about 10 kilograms</u>, but it is <u>strong</u> enough to support the body and hold it <u>upright</u>.

This excerpt from paragraph 3 describes the femur:

> . . . Other bones, such as the femur, or thighbone, help support the body. The femur is the <u>longest bone in the body</u>. It is an average of <u>48 centimeters long</u>, and it supports the weight of the body as we walk and run.

3 | Sample paragraph

My hand measures about 8 centimeters wide and 16 centimeters long. It has a palm with thin lines in it. It also has five fingers of different lengths. The longest finger is 7.5 centimeters and the shortest is 5.5 centimeters. The color of my hand is light brown, and the skin is smooth and a little dry. My hand is very flexible, and it can bend in different ways. This allows me to grab things and hold on to them.

3 THE HEART AND THE CIRCULATORY SYSTEM

Preparing to read (Student's Book pg. 176)

BUILDING BACKGROUND KNOWLEDGE ABOUT THE TOPIC

2 | Sample answers

1 The circulatory system transports materials to and from all the cells in the body.

2 The three main parts of the circulatory system are blood, the heart, and blood vessels. The heart pumps blood through the body. Blood vessels are small tubes that the blood travels through. Blood delivers oxygen, water, and nutrients, and it picks up waste products.

CONDUCTING AN EXPERIMENT

1–3 Answers will vary. (An average resting pulse rate is between 60 and 100 beats per minute. After running in place, pulse rates will be higher than resting rates.)

Now read

Refer to pages xi–xii of this Teacher's Manual for suggestions about ways in which students can read the text.

After you read (Student's Book pg. 179)

Task 1 TEST TAKING: ANSWERING MULTIPLE CHOICE QUESTIONS

Answers

1	b	**6**	d
2	d	**7**	a
3	d	**8**	c
4	b	**9**	c
5	a	**10**	b

Task 2 SEQUENCING

1 | **Answers**

_5_ Blood flows to the left ventricle.

_7_ Blood returns to the heart through the right atrium.

_2_ Blood flows to the right ventricle.

_3_ Blood travels through the pulmonary artery to the lungs.

_1_ Blood enters the heart through the right atrium.

_6_ Blood travels through the aorta to all parts of the body.

_4_ Blood picks up oxygen and returns to the heart through the left atrium.

2 | The arrows drawn on the diagram should follow the path shown in Figure 8.3 on Student's Book page 177.

Task 3 NOTE TAKING: FROM HIGHLIGHTING TO OUTLINING

1 | **Sample highlighting and notes**

carry blood

3 types

heart to body

body to heart

connect arteries + veins

Every time the heart beats, it pushes blood through the body's blood vessels. There are more than 96,000 kilometers of blood vessels inside the body. If they were stretched out, they would circle Earth more than two times. Arteries are blood vessels that carry blood away from the heart to all parts of the body. Veins are blood vessels that carry blood from the body back to the heart. Arteries and veins are connected by tiny blood vessels called capillaries.

2 | **Sample answers**

III. Blood vessels

    A. Arteries: carry blood away from heart to body

    B. Veins: carry blood from body back to heart

    C. Capillaries: connect arteries & veins

3 | **Sample answers**

Your heart works hard. It started beating before you were born, ~~strong heart muscle + clean arteries~~ and it will continue to beat for your whole life. Having a healthy heart means that the heart muscle is strong and that the arteries are clean and open. If the arteries that supply blood to the heart become blocked, it could cause a heart attack. Each year, millions of people die of heart attacks. Therefore, it is very important to keep your heart healthy. One of the best things you can do is to avoid smoking. Exercise and a good diet can also help keep the heart in good shape.

[margin notes: strong heart muscle + clean arteries; don't smoke, exercise, good diet]

VI. Heart health
   A. Healthy heart = strong heart muscle & clean, open arteries
   B. Blocked arteries can → heart attack
   C. To keep heart healthy: don't smoke, do exercise, eat good diet

Task 4 LANGUAGE FOCUS: PREPOSITIONS OF DIRECTION

1 | **Answers**

par. 4: . . . The flow of blood works in this way: Blood from all over the body enters the heart through the top right chamber, called the right atrium. This blood flows to the bottom right chamber, called the right ventricle. The heart then pumps the blood out of the right ventricle, through the pulmonary artery, into the lungs.

par. 5: In the lungs, the blood picks up oxygen, and then it returns to the heart through the left atrium. Next, the blood flows to the left ventricle. The heart then pumps the blood out of the left ventricle into the aorta, which is the largest artery in the body. The blood travels through the aorta and other smaller arteries to all parts of the body, delivering oxygen to all the cells. The blood then travels through capillaries to veins that lead back to the heart. From the veins, the blood goes into the right atrium of the heart to begin the process again. The whole cycle takes about 30 seconds.

2 | **Answers**

   1 Arteries carry blood away from the heart to all parts of the body.
   2 Blood travels through blood vessels.
   3 Blood carries oxygen from the lungs to all the cells in the body.
   4 Dr. Barnard transplanted a new heart into the body of Louis Washkansky.
   5 Blood travels through capillaries to veins.
   6 The heart pumps blood out of the left ventricle and into the aorta.

3 | **Sample sentences**

   1 The brain receives messages from the body through the spinal cord.
   2 The eyes send messages from the outside world to the brain.
   3 The lungs receive blood from the heart.
   4 Blood carries nutrients to the body's cells.

Task 5 BUILDING VOCABULARY: HAVING FUN WITH WORDS

Sample answers

1 bones (other words name parts of the circulatory system)
2 lungs (other words name materials that blood delivers to the body's cells)
3 aorta (other words name chambers of the heart)
4 body (other words name organs)
5 blood (other words name blood vessels)
6 smoking (other words name things that are good for the heart)

Task 6 WRITING A DESCRIPTION

1 | **Sample answers**

Key features of the heart	Notes
size	about as big as a fist
weight	about 300 grams
color	mostly red
main parts	right atrium, right ventricle, left atrium, left ventricle

2 | **Sample paragraph**

The human heart is not a large organ. In fact, the heart is about as big as a fist, and it weighs about 300 grams. Just like other muscles in the body, the heart is mostly red in color. It has four main parts: the right atrium, the right ventricle, the left atrium, and the left ventricle.

Chapter 8 WRITING ASSIGNMENT (Student's Book page 183).

1 | **Sample answers**

Facts about the human liver:
• weighs about 1.5 kilograms
• color is reddish-brown
• consists of four main parts, called lobes

3 | **Sample paragraph**

The Human Liver

The human liver has several special features and functions. It is the largest internal organ in the human body. In fact, it is about as big as a football. An average liver weighs about 1.5 kilograms. This soft, reddish-brown organ is located below the heart and next to the stomach. It has four main parts, called lobes. In addition, the liver is one of the few organs that can rebuild itself if it gets damaged. One key function of the liver is to help the body get rid of harmful substances. It is also a storage place for some vitamins and minerals. These are just a few of the reasons why the liver is one of the most important organs in the body.

Living Longer, Living Better?

1 LIFE EXPECTANCY: FROM 25 to 100+

Preparing to read (Student's Book pg. 184)

EXAMINING GRAPHIC MATERIAL

2 | **Sample answers**
1 The x-axis shows names of countries; the y-axis shows years of age.
2 *Life expectancy* means "the number of years that a person or group of people will probably live."
3 A baby born in China in 2008 would probably live 73 years.
4 Andorra had the highest life expectancy in 2008.
5 Swaziland had the lowest life expectancy.
6 Answers will vary.

THINKING ABOUT THE TOPIC BEFORE YOU READ

Students are not expected to know the answers to these items. It is simply a way to get them to start thinking about the issues addressed in the text.

Sample answers
1 Life expectancy is higher in richer countries because they have better living conditions, better nutrition, and better medical care. Life expectancy is lower in countries with frequent wars.
2 Answers will vary. (In 2008, the average life expectancy for the world was 66 years).
3 Answers will vary. (Experts predict that in 2050, the average life expectancy will be 95 years. This is because health care keeps improving in many parts of the world.)

Now read

Refer to pages xi–xii of this Teacher's Manual for suggestions about ways in which students can read the text.

After you read (Student's Book pg. 187)

Task 1 READING FOR MAIN IDEAS AND DETAILS

1 | **Answers**

<u>M</u> 1   <u>M</u> 6
<u>D</u> 2   <u>D</u> 7
<u>D</u> 3   <u>D</u> 8
<u>M</u> 4   <u>M</u> 9
<u>D</u> 5   <u>D</u> 10

2 | **Answer**

Life expectancy has increased very quickly in the past 100 years for three reasons.

3,4 | **Answers**

Main ideas	Supporting details
1 A healthy way of life helps people live longer.	**3** Exercising and managing stress help people live healthier lives. **5** Smoking can reduce the number of years people live.
	• Working in a safe, clean environment can increase the number of years a person lives.
6 Life expectancy in the world increased as living conditions became cleaner.	**7** Dirty living conditions can lead to the spread of diseases. **10** Most people today live in a cleaner environment than in the past.
	• In the past, living conditions in most of the world were unsanitary.
9 Better nutrition is one reason life expectancy has increased.	**8** Food storage practices, such as refrigeration, help people eat better all year. **2** In the past, people got sick because they could not always eat a balanced diet.
	• Today, more people eat a balanced diet because they know more about health and nutrition.

Task 2 APPLYING WHAT YOU HAVE READ

1 | **Answers**

The following items should be checked: 1, 2, 4, 6, 7, 9

2 | **Sample answers**

1 Healthy habits include getting seven to eight hours of sleep each night, having regular medical checkups, and spending time with friends and family.

Unhealthy habits include sleeping only a few hours each night, eating a lot of junk food, and not getting enough exercise.

2–4 Answers will vary.

Task 3 BUILDING VOCABULARY: SUFFIXES

1 | Answers

1 operation
2 sanitation
3 connection
4 prevention

5 improvement
6 transportation
7 refrigeration
8 management

2 | Answers

1 adj.
2 n.
3 n.

4 adj.
5 adj.
6 n.

3 | Answers

adj. 1 environmental

n. 2 nutrition

adj. 3 personal

n. 4 environment

adj. 5 medical

4 | Sample sentences

- (n.) The public <u>transportation</u> in my city is very good. There are many buses, trains, and taxicabs that people use to get around town.

- (adj.) Eating <u>nutritious</u> food is one way to stay healthy.

- (v.) Sometimes doctors have to <u>operate</u> on people to help them get better.

Task 4 LANGUAGE FOCUS: ADVERBS OF MANNER

1 | Answers

1 A lack of sanitation causes diseases to spread <u>quickly</u>.

2 Improvements in sanitation helped life expectancy to rise <u>rapidly</u>.

3 Thanks to ships and planes, we can <u>easily</u> transport food long distances.

4 Many centenarians exercise <u>regularly</u>.

2 | Sample answers

1 The student conducted the experiment carefully.

2 The doctor talked kindly to the patient.

3 The scientist cleaned the microscope quickly.

4 The researcher walked into the room quietly.

Task 5 UNDERSTANDING A BAR GRAPH

1 | Sample sentences

1 There were more than 17,000 centenarians in China in 2007–2008.

2 Japan had approximately 30,000 more centenarians than Cuba did in 2007–2008.

2 | Sample bar graph

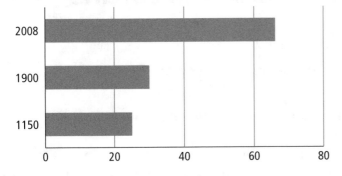

3,4 | Answers and bar graphs will vary.

Task 6 WRITING AN EXPLANATION

1 | Answers

   1 Exercise helps people live longer, healthier lives because it helps prevent many diseases. It also makes the heart and lungs stronger.

   2 <u>One reason is that</u> regular exercise can help prevent many diseases. <u>The other reason is that</u> exercise makes the heart and lungs stronger.

2 | Answers

There are three reasons for an increase in life expectancy: improvements in sanitation, improvements in nutrition, and healthier lifestyles.

3 | Answers

Highlighting will vary. Check to make sure that students' highlighting is limited to important information.

4 | Sample paragraph

   There are three reasons why life expectancy has increased in recent years. One reason is that living conditions are more sanitary today. In the past, people did not often take baths or wash their hands. However, most people today know it is important to keep clean in order to stay healthy. Another reason is improvement in nutrition. Today, many people eat a better diet than they did in the past because they can store nutritious food, such as milk, eggs, and fish, in refrigerators. People also know more about the nutrients our bodies need to stay healthy. The third reason people can expect to live longer is that many people have healthier lifestyles. For example, these days many people do not smoke. They also work fewer hours, and they spend more time exercising and resting. Therefore, thanks to cleaner living conditions, better diets, and healthier lifestyles, people are living longer today than they did in the past.

2 ADVANCES IN THE FIELD OF MEDICINE

Preparing to read (Student's Book pg. 192)

BUILDING VOCABULARY: PREVIEWING KEY WORDS

1 | Sample answers

   1 Some other diseases are mumps, tetanus, whooping cough, cancer, and diabetes.

   2 Antibiotics and vaccines are medicines.

   3 Other things that can help sick people get better include rest, healthy food, and operations.

PREVIEWING KEY PARTS OF A TEXT

1 | Sample answers

   1 The text is about improvements in medicine that have helped people live longer and healthier lives.

   2 The text discusses antibiotics, vaccines, and new developments in surgery.

2 | Answers

   F **1**

   T **2**

   T **3**

   F **4**

   T **5**

Now read

Refer to pages xi–xii of this Teacher's Manual for suggestions about ways in which students can read the text.

After you read (Student's Book pg. 195)

Task 1 TEST TAKING: ANSWERING A VARIETY OF TEST QUESTIONS

1 | Answers

   F **1**

   T **2**

   T **3**

   T **4**

   F **5**

2 | Answers

1 b
2 d
3 c
4 a
5 b
6 c

3 | Sample answers

1 Antibiotics and vaccines are both medicines. Antibiotics help people after they get sick from an infection, but vaccines prevent people from getting sick from certain diseases.

2 When a person has an organ transplant, a doctor takes out the sick organ and replaces it with a new, healthy one.

3 Some people cannot afford to see a doctor or to buy medicine when they need it.

Task 2 BUILDING VOCABULARY: USING KEY WORDS

1 | Answers

1 vaccine (vaccination)
2 transplant
3 epidemic
4 antibiotic
5 surgery

Task 3 LANGUAGE FOCUS: TIME EXPRESSIONS AND VERB TENSES

1 | Answers

In the past, diseases killed millions of people. More than 20 million people in Asia, Africa, North America, and Europe died in the 1918 flu epidemic. However, far fewer people died in the flu epidemics of 1957 and 1968. This was mainly because of the development of antibiotics and vaccines. Today, doctors use antibiotics and vaccines to treat and prevent many different illnesses. Doctors hope that, in the future, they will make more progress in the fight against diseases such as cancer and AIDS.

Paragraph	Time expression (circled in text)	Verb (underlined in text)
par. 1	Today In earlier times Since the mid-twentieth century	results might have caused have helped save
par. 2	In the past 1918 In the twentieth century World War II Now today	killed died developed was first . . . used use die
par. 3	Today since 1977 in the 1950s today	provide have (not) been started get sick, die
par. 4	today In the past Today	are living could (not) survive are able to live
par. 5	In the past Today	died might receive
par. 6	in 2002	died

3 | Answers

>   In the twentieth century, polio ~~is~~ ^{was} one of the most terrible childhood
>
> diseases. Each year, polio struck thousands of people, most of them
>
> children, and made some of them unable to walk. In the 1950s, a polio
>
> vaccine ~~will be~~ ^{was} developed. ~~In the past~~ ^{Today}, most of the world's people do not
>
> get this disease. However, in a few countries, there are still people who
>
> suffer from polio. In the future, doctors hope that polio, like smallpox,
>
> ~~disappeared~~ ^{will disappear} completely.

4 | Sample sentences

1 Five years ago, I liked to play soccer.
   Today, I like to play basketball.
   In 10 years, I think I will try to play golf or tennis.

2 In the past, my home was near the ocean.
   These days, I live far away from the coast.
   In the future, I think I will live near the ocean again.

Task 4 NOTE TAKING: CHOOSING A TECHNIQUE THAT WORKS FOR YOU

1 | Answers will vary. Check to make sure that students' highlighting and note taking are limited to important information.

Task 5 THINKING CRITICALLY ABOUT THE TOPIC

1–4 | Answers will vary.

Task 6 UNDERSTANDING CAUSE AND EFFECT

1 | **Answers**

  1 Some people do not get vaccines because they are too expensive.
  2 Infections can cause death.
  3 Another reason many people died in the twentieth century was smallpox epidemics.
  4 Advances in the medical field often result in more people living longer.

2 | **Answers**

  1 main idea: why hearts fail
  2 The paragraph mainly discusses causes.
  3 The writer discusses three causes: bad habits, viruses, and problems that a person is born with.

  4

> There are three major reasons for heart failure. First, a person's heart may fail because of bad habits, such as smoking, eating fatty foods, and not exercising. Viruses can also cause heart failure. For example, the coxsackie virus can damage the heart muscle and cause it to fail. In addition, heart problems that a person is born with can result in heart failure. Doctors are studying these three causes because they want to improve the treatment of their patients.

3 SEEKING BALANCE IN THE NATURAL WORLD

Preparing to read (Student's Book pg. 200)

THINKING ABOUT THE TOPIC BEFORE YOU READ

Students are not expected to know the answers to these items. It is simply a way to get them to start thinking about the issues addressed in the text.

Sample answers

  1 Yes, I think the natural world has changed in the past 100 years. I think the changes have been mostly negative, because we have lost a lot of nature. For example, many types of plants and animals are now endangered or extinct.

2 • I think the natural world will be worse than it is now. In fact, there may be very little nature left in 100 years.

• I think the natural world will be better because people will know more about ways to protect nature.

3 To protect the natural world, people are recycling, planting new trees, driving hybrid cars, and using clean, renewable sources of energy, such as wind and solar power.

INCREASING YOUR READING SPEED

1–3 Although much of the emphasis in this text is on reading comprehension, increasing speed is also an important goal for academic learners. Assist students by writing the start time on the board. You can ask them to write down their own finishing times, or you can write the time on the board as each minute passes. Then have students calculate their reading rates.

4 **Answers**
  1 good
  2 more
  3 Pollution
  4 helped

Now read

Refer to pages xi–xii of this Teacher's Manual for suggestions about ways in which students can read the text.

After you read (Student's Book pg. 203)

Task 1 ASKING FOR CLARIFICATION

1,2 Answers will vary. For examples of clarification questions, refer to page 58 of this Teacher's Manual.

Task 2 NOTE TAKING: CHOOSING A TECHNIQUE THAT WORKS FOR YOU

2 Answers will vary. Check to make sure that students' highlighting and note taking are limited to important information.

Task 3 TEST TAKING: WRITING YOUR OWN TEST QUESTIONS

1 **Answers**
Answers will vary. Test questions should include true/false, multiple choice, and short-answer questions.

Task 4 LANGUAGE FOCUS: INFINITIVES

1 | Answers

People are trying <u>to protect</u> nature in various ways. Some people are cleaning up the water and the air by building wind energy farms, water treatment centers, and electric cars. Others are trying <u>to restore</u> damaged habitats, grow more trees, and preserve, or save, endangered plants and animals. For example, in the 1970s, the bald eagle and the American peregrine falcon were both endangered. The U.S. government made laws <u>to try</u> <u>to protect</u> the birds. As a result, today these bird species are not endangered anymore, and they are living successfully in their natural habitats.

2 | Sample answers

1 In the twentieth century, the population began to <u>grow</u>.

2 The more people there are on Earth, the more <u>homes</u> they need to <u>build</u>.

3 Some people are trying <u>to clean up the water</u> / <u>to plant trees</u> / <u>to change daily habits</u> / <u>to restore damaged habitats</u> in order to preserve the natural world.

4 In order to protect nature, more people should try <u>to recycle</u> / <u>to save water</u> / <u>to plant trees</u>.

5 To protect our planet, I want <u>to clean up the parks in my town</u> / <u>to learn more about environmental issues</u> / <u>to plant a garden</u>.

Task 5 BUILDING VOCABULARY: SYNONYMS AND ANTONYMS

1 | Answers

<u>b</u> 1

<u>e</u> 2

<u>c</u> 3

<u>a</u> 4

<u>d</u> 5

2 | Answers

<u>c</u> 1

<u>e</u> 2

<u>d</u> 3

<u>b</u> 4

<u>a</u> 5

Task 6 THINKING CRITICALLY ABOUT THE TOPIC

Sample answers

1 The biggest problems for the natural world include overpopulation, pollution, and deforestation.

2 I think governments should make stricter laws to protect the environment, punish people and companies who break environmental protection laws, and spend more money for research on renewable sources of energy and climate change.

3 To protect the planet, I recycle paper and plastic, and I try not to use too much water. I also drive a hybrid car. I could walk and take public transportation more often.

Task 7 CONDUCTING A SURVEY

1,2 | Answers and bar graphs will vary.

Task 8 WRITING ABOUT CAUSE AND EFFECT

2 | **Answers**

par. 2: Today, people are living longer, and (as a result,) there are more people on Earth than ever before.

par. 3: (As a result,) much of the water in our oceans, rivers, lakes, and ground is polluted . . .

par. 4: Air pollution (causes) more than 2 million deaths each year. This (leads to) global warming and the environmental problems it causes.

par. 7: (As a result,) these birds are not endangered anymore, and they are living successfully in their natural habitats.

4 | **Sample answers**

Causes of deforestation	Effects of deforestation
1 need for farmland	1 drought
2 need for wood to build houses	2 loss of plant and animal habitats

5 | **Sample sentences**

1 When people cut down trees for wood to build houses, it can lead to deforestation.

2 One effect of deforestation is drought.

7 | **Answers**

1 main idea of the first paragraph: the causes of deforestation

2 main idea of the second paragraph: the effects of deforestation

3 The writer discusses three causes: construction, the need for new land to grow food, and the need for fuel.

4 The writer discusses two effects: a decrease in biodiversity and climate problems.

5

> There are several <u>causes</u> of deforestation in the world today. All of the
> <u>causes</u> are related to the growing population of the world. <u>One major cause</u>
> is construction. People need more and more wood to build homes and
> furniture. <u>Therefore</u>, they are cutting down more trees. <u>Another reason</u> for
> deforestation is the need for new land to grow food. In addition, people
> need fuel. Many people are using trees as firewood for cooking and heating.
> <u>For these reasons</u>, deforestation continues on our planet.
>
> Our planet suffers from deforestation in important ways. First, cutting
> down forests <u>causes</u> a decrease in biodiversity. In fact, many species are
> now endangered or extinct <u>because of</u> deforestation. Cutting down trees
> can also <u>result in</u> environmental problems. When forests are cut down, they
> can no longer absorb (take in and hold) rain. This often <u>leads to</u> periods of
> flooding, followed by drought, or extreme dryness. These examples make it
> clear that the <u>effects</u> of deforestation on Earth are very serious.

Chapter 9 WRITING ASSIGNMENT (Student's Book pg. 207)

1 | **Sample paragraphs**

Climate Change: Reasons and Results

Sometimes there are natural reasons for climate change on Earth. For example, the 1815 eruption of Mount Tambora in Indonesia changed weather patterns around the world. However, recent changes in climate are mainly the result of human activity. One reason for these changes is our increasing use of fossil fuels, such as oil, gas, and coal. As our planet's population grows, more and more people drive cars, fly in airplanes, and use electricity. When we burn more fossil fuel, it causes an increase in the amount of carbon dioxide in the air. Carbon dioxide is one of the gases that keeps heat in the atmosphere. When there is more carbon dioxide in the air, our planet gets warmer. This is called global warming. Another reason for recent climate change is deforestation. When forests are cut down for human needs, such as land for agriculture and building materials, it decreases the number of trees on our planet. Trees are important because they remove carbon dioxide from the air during photosynthesis. Therefore, if there are fewer trees, there will be more carbon dioxide. Clearly, burning more fossil fuels and deforestation have both led to climate change.

The effects of climate change on our planet are serious. For example, as Earth grows warmer, glaciers begin to melt faster. In 2007, scientists found that glaciers were melting three times more quickly than they did in the 1980s. When glaciers melt, ocean levels rise. In fact, in the past one hundred years, ocean levels around the world rose up to 20 centimeters. Scientists predict that ocean levels could rise as much as 60 more centimeters in the next one hundred years. When ocean levels rise, the flooding of coastal areas can kill people and cause great damage to the land, homes, and businesses. Global warming also results in changes in weather patterns around the world. Some areas become colder, and others get hotter. Some areas get wetter, and others get drier. For example, since the 1970s, very dry areas across the planet more than doubled. Melting glaciers, rising ocean levels, and changing weather patterns are just a few examples of how human actions affect climate on Earth.

Additional Ideas for Unit 4

Key topics in this unit include the common characteristics of all living things, plant life and animal life. The unit pays special attention to humans, including discussions of the human body (the brain, skeletal and muscular systems, the heart and circulatory system), life expectancy, and the challenges facing the natural world as a result of human activity.

1 | If possible, have students examine slides of plant and animal cells under a microscope. Have them identify the parts of the cell and discuss what they see.

2 | Have students work in small groups and categorize the plant life and animal life in their neighborhoods. Students can create posters, including information such as the following: Is the animal a vertebrate or an invertebrate? Is the plant a seed or seedless plant? Is the plant or animal an endangered species or not? Ask students to illustrate the posters with photos or drawings of the organisms.

3 | Have students research a medicinal plant, such as arnica or peppermint, and share their findings with the class. Have students bring in a sample of the plant, if possible.

4 | Have students choose an endangered or extinct animal and do research on why it became endangered / extinct. Have them find out if any progress is being made to save the endangered animals.

5 | Ask students to observe two or more animals and take notes on how they communicate with each other. Have students report their findings to the class.

6 | Have students research a famous medical clinic or medical pioneer. Ask them to share the information in a brief class presentation and / or a one-paragraph report.

7 | Ask students to interview a person who is 80 or older. Have students create four to six interview questions about the person's lifestyle, attitudes, and so on. Have students compare their results and discuss possible reasons for longevity.

8 | Have the class brainstorm a list of the things they can do in their community to help protect the natural world.

9 | Create a quiz-type game (like *Jeopardy!* or *Family Feud*). First, have students create categories based on topics in this unit (plant life, animal life, the human body, the environment, etc.). Then ask students to contribute questions (designated easy, medium, and hard) for each category. Select (and edit, if necessary) appropriate questions. Students can play the game in teams.

10 | Have students research the Hudson River Sloop Clearwater organization, founded by Pete Seeger to clean up the pollution in New York State's Hudson River. Students can also find and share the lyrics of some of Seeger's songs on environmental issues.

Unit **1** CONTENT QUIZ

PART 1 True/False Questions (25 points)

Decide if the following statements are true (*T*) or false (*F*).

_____ **1** Terrestrial planets are made of gases.

_____ **2** The hydrosphere is all the water on Earth.

_____ **3** The three main types of rocks are lava, magma, and igneous.

_____ **4** Extinct volcanoes can erupt in the future.

_____ **5** Scientists cannot predict or stop earthquakes.

PART 2 Multiple Choice Questions (25 points)

Circle the best answer from the list of choices.

1 The sun is a _____.
   a planet
   b star
   c moon
   d plutoid

2 All the living things on Earth are part of the _____.
   a lithosphere
   b hydrosphere
   c atmosphere
   d biosphere

3 At convergent boundaries _____.
   a tectonic plates move past each other
   b tectonic plates stop moving
   c tectonic plates move toward each other
   d tectonic plates move away from each other

4 Most volcanoes are located _____.
   a in the Atlantic Ocean
   b around the Pacific Plate
   c in California
   d over hotspots

5 Earthquakes are caused by _____.
   a tectonic plate movement
   b human behavior
   c rocks on Earth's surface
   d shaking buildings

PART 3 Short-answer Questions (50 points)

In one or two sentences, write a short answer to each of the following questions:

1 Describe our solar system.

2 Give an example of how Earth's systems are interconnected.

3 Choose one rock type and explain how it forms.

4 Explain Wegener's continental drift theory.

5 Name one positive and one negative effect of volcanoes.

Unit **2** CONTENT QUIZ

PART 1 True/False Questions (25 points)

Decide if the following statements are true (*T*) or false (*F*).

_____ **1** Water covers about 50 percent of our planet.

_____ **2** Glaciers do not move.

_____ **3** The amount of salinity in an ocean depends on the amount of evaporation and the amount of freshwater added.

_____ **4** Wind causes surface currents.

_____ **5** Tsunamis are warm ocean currents.

PART 2 Multiple Choice Questions (25 points)

Circle the best answer from the list of choices.

1 Which one of the following is not a step in the water cycle?
   a precipitation
   b eruption
   c condensation
   d evaporation

2 Which one of the following is true about rivers?
   a They are surrounded on all sides by land.
   b They are an important source of salt water.
   c They are also called aquifers.
   d They carve V-shaped valleys.

3 Which one of the following is the smallest ocean?
   a the Arctic Ocean
   b the Atlantic Ocean
   c the Indian Ocean
   d the Pacific Ocean

4 Which one of the following is not true about currents?
   a They stop warm water from becoming too hot.
   b They stop cold water from becoming too cold.
   c They always move from east to west.
   d They can influence climate.

5 Tsunamis
   a are caused by wind.
   b move slowly.
   c happen only in the Pacific Ocean.
   d can kill people.

PART 3 Short-answer Questions (50 points)

In one or two sentences, write a short answer to each of the following questions:

1 Billions of people live on our planet, and they use a lot of water every day. Why don't we ever run out of water?

2 Explain one similarity and one difference between a river and an ocean.

3 How does a glacier form?

4 Why does ocean water near the equator usually have high levels of salinity?

5 What is a tsunami?

Unit **3** CONTENT QUIZ

PART 1 True/False Questions (25 points)

Decide if the following statements are true (*T*) or false (*F*).

_____ **1** Nitrogen is the most common gas in the atmosphere.

_____ **2** When you see stratus clouds, the weather is usually good and the sky is blue.

_____ **3** Polar climates are very cold and very dry.

_____ **4** Tornadoes form over warm ocean waters.

_____ **5** Another name for a hurricane is *typhoon*.

PART 2 Multiple Choice Questions (25 points)

Circle the best answer from the list of choices.

1 Which of the following is not a gas in the atmosphere?
   a oxygen
   b ozone
   c carbon dioxide
   d radium

2 Which of the following is not a layer of the atmosphere?
   a stratosphere
   b mesosphere
   c unisphere
   d exosphere

3 Which of the following is true about cumulus clouds?
   a They are high-level clouds.
   b They are sometimes called fog.
   c You often see them right before a storm.
   d They are fluffy and white.

4 What type of climate do the following sentences describe?

   This climate is neither very cold nor very hot. It has some rain but not a lot.

   a tropical
   b mild
   c dry
   d polar

5 Which country has the most tornadoes each year?
   a The United States
   b Canada
   c China
   d Ecuador

PART 3 Short-answer Questions (50 points)

In one or two sentences, write a short answer to each of the following questions:

1 Give two reasons why people need the atmosphere.

2 Describe one type of cloud. Include details about what it looks like and what it can tell you about the weather.

3 What is climate?

4 Explain at least one similarity and one difference between a thunderstorm and a tornado.

5 Name the three main parts of a hurricane. Which part contains the most rain and the strongest winds?

Academic Encounters: The Natural World © Cambridge University Press 2009 Photocopiable

Unit **4** CONTENT QUIZ

PART 1 True/False Questions (25 points)

Decide if the following statements are true (*T*) or false (*F*).

_____ **1** All plants grow from seeds.

_____ **2** Vertebrates are animals that have a backbone.

_____ **3** The heart controls everything we do.

_____ **4** Bones are heavy and strong.

_____ **5** Human actions have caused changes in the natural world.

PART 2 Multiple Choice Questions (25 points)

Circle the best answer from the list of choices.

1 Which of the following is not an organism?
  a a person
  b a dog
  c a cloud
  d a tree

2 Which of the following is not a symbiotic relationship?
  a commensalism
  b communication
  c parasitism
  d mutualism

3 The _____ is the largest part of the brain, and it controls most of our thinking and speaking.
  a brain stem
  b aorta
  c cerebellum
  d cerebrum

4 Doctors often give people _____ to prevent them from getting certain diseases.
  a vaccines
  b transplants
  c antibiotics
  d polio

5 Which of the following is not a problem facing the natural world?
  a deforestation
  b air pollution
  c water pollution
  d conservation

PART 3 Short-answer Questions (50 points)

In one or two sentences, write a short answer to each of the following questions:

1 Explain the meaning of this sentence: *Life on our planet is very diverse.*

2 Give two reasons that many plant and animal species are losing their natural habitats.

3 What are blood vessels?

4 Give two reasons that life expectancy has increased rapidly in the past 100 years.

5 Name one problem that shows the natural world is out of balance. What can people do to improve this situation?

Unit **1** CONTENT QUIZ ANSWERS

PART 1

<u>F</u> **1**
<u>T</u> **2**
<u>F</u> **3**
<u>F</u> **4**
<u>T</u> **5**

PART 2

<u>b</u> **1**
<u>d</u> **2**
<u>c</u> **3**
<u>b</u> **4**
<u>a</u> **5**

PART 3

1 The response can include any of the following: the sun at the center of our solar system; the eight planets and Pluto; the contrast between terrestrial and gas giant planets; and the idea that planets orbit the sun and moons orbit planets.

2 The response should include one of the following examples (or similar examples) of how two or more systems are interconnected:
- Humans are part of the biosphere, but they live on the lithosphere.
- Humans are part of the biosphere, but they pollute the atmosphere when they fly on airplanes.
- Lakes are part of the hydrosphere, but they provide the living things of the biosphere with the water they need.

3 The response should discuss one of the following rock types:
- Igneous rock forms when magma rises up through Earth's crust and cools. Sometimes magma cools under the surface of Earth, and sometimes it erupts from a volcano as lava and cools on the surface.
- Sedimentary rock forms when small pieces of rock break off and form a layer of sediment at the bottom of a river or ocean. Over time, more layers of sediment form on top, and the weight from all the layers presses the sediment so tightly together that it eventually becomes solid sedimentary rock.
- Metamorphic rock forms when the heat and pressure deep inside Earth change one type of rock into another.

4 Wegener's continental drift theory suggests that millions of years ago, Earth had just one giant continent, Pangaea. Over time, Pangaea broke apart, and the pieces drifted, or moved, to where the continents are today.

5 Positive effects of volcanoes include the formation of new mountains, new islands, and new land. Negative effects include the destruction of towns and cities, the death of many people, and dramatic and harmful weather changes.

Unit 2 CONTENT QUIZ ANSWERS

PART 1

F 1

F 2

T 3

T 4

F 5

PART 2

b 1

d 2

a 3

c 4

d 5

PART 3

1 We do not run out of water because nature keeps recycling water in a process called the water cycle.

2 The response should state one similarity and one difference between a river and an ocean. Similarities can include the following: They are both surface water features. They are both part of the water cycle on Earth. They both provide food and recreation for people. Differences can include the following: Rivers contain freshwater, but oceans contain salt water. Rivers are narrow, but oceans are wide. Oceans are bigger than rivers. Oceans have waves and currents, but rivers do not.

3 A glacier starts to form when snow falls and builds up layers that press down on each other until they become ice. The thick layers of ice become a glacier when they become so heavy that they begin to slide over the ground.

4 Near the equator, the heat of the sun causes a lot of ocean water to evaporate, and it leaves the salt behind. In addition, it does not rain much, so there is not a lot of freshwater to dilute, or weaken, the salty water.

5 A tsunami is a giant wave that forms when there is an underwater earthquake or volcanic eruption. When these fast, powerful waves reach land, they rise up high in the air and crash down, causing damage and killing people.

Unit 3 CONTENT QUIZ ANSWERS

PART 1

T 1
F 2
T 3
F 4
T 5

PART 2

d 1
c 2
d 3
b 4
a 5

PART 3

1 The response should include two of the following reasons: We need the oxygen (or breathable air) to keep us alive. The nitrogen in the air is necessary for the plants that we grow for food. The atmosphere acts like a shield and protects us from objects that fall from space. The ozone in the air protects us from the harmful rays of the sun.

2 The response should discuss one of the following types of clouds:
   - Cumulus clouds are fluffy, white, low-level clouds. When you see cumulus clouds, the weather is usually good, and the sky is blue.
   - Cirrus clouds are thin, wispy, white clouds high in the sky. When you see cirrus clouds, it usually means that stormy weather is coming.
   - Stratus clouds look like thick, gray, shapeless blankets that cover most of the sky. When you see these low-level clouds, you might soon see rain.

3 Climate is the average weather conditions of an area over a long period of time (at least 30 years). It includes the average temperature and the average amount of precipitation.

4 The response should state one similarity and one difference. Similarities can include the following: Both can cause damage and death. Both occur all over the world. Both are usually short storms. Differences can include the following: Most thunderstorms are harmless, but tornadoes are usually dangerous. Flooding is the most dangerous part of thunderstorms, but powerful winds are the biggest danger in a tornado.

5 The three main parts of a hurricane are the eye, the eyewall, and the spiral rain bands. The eyewall contains the strongest winds and the most rain.

Unit 4 CONTENT QUIZ ANSWERS

PART 1

_F_ 1
_T_ 2
_F_ 3
_F_ 4
_T_ 5

PART 2

_c_ 1
_b_ 2
_d_ 3
_a_ 4
_d_ 5

PART 3

1 The sentence means that there are many different species of plants and animals on Earth. They are all different shapes and sizes, and they live in a wide variety of places.

2 The response should include two of the following reasons: natural disasters; pollution; human activities, such as deforestation and the development of land; and environmental changes, such as global warming.

3 Blood vessels are small tubes that carry blood through the body.

4 The response should include two of the following: improvements in sanitation; improvements in nutrition; healthier lifestyles; and medical advances, including antibiotics, vaccines, and developments in surgery.

5 The response should include one of the following problems and one thing people can do about it:

- air pollution: walk / bike more and drive less; use public transportation; drive an electric car; use wind or solar power; plant trees and gardens
- water pollution: don't dump garbage in water; build water treatment plants
- loss of plants' and animals' natural habitats: limit deforestation; restore damaged habitats by planting more trees; clean up polluted air and water

The response might also include the idea that people should try to learn more about environmental protection.